GAY AND LESBIAN

THE TRUTH!

By CLEMY LEE

TABLE OF CONTENTS

ACKNOWLEDGEMENTS

Thank You Jehovah God

Thank you Jehovah God for making your knowledge and wisdom available to us all.

Thanks for showing me your ways, at a very early age, and strengthening my faith, that would chasten and protect me every day, even during those times when I would stray.

Thanks for the Prophets and the Saints, whom I myself am not able to thank, due to the difference in our times, as the biblical is very distant from mine, but the prophets never broke stride in giving us examples to live by, as even they were being tried, and did not know if they'd survive.

Thanks for Jesus from us all; who paid the ultimate cost, as he was nailed to the cross, for people he never even saw, but thankfully his life would not be lost.

Thanks for your salvation, even for these perverse ungrateful nations, and all of their wicked imaginations, which proves that your love has no limitations.

Thank you for my Mother, she really loved you like no other, she did her best to get it right, and made certain that you were in our lives.

Thank you for my wife, who humbled herself to do what's right, which made it easier in this life to fight the good fight.

So Thank You Jehovah God!

I

INTRODUCTION

This book was written to enlighten the world of things that were meant to be, but have somehow gotten lost over the years as society moves forward in its attempt to become wiser, stronger and more independent in its ability to govern itself. I will point out for you, the appropriate manner in which we should be conducting ourselves opposed to the way in which we are conducting ourselves. In this book, I will touch on just about every aspect of life, with factual documentation for your review. After you have read this book, you will walk away with a greater sense of being. Some of the things you learn will hurt, some will feel good, and some of it you already know, but probably just aren't ready to face. It is very easy for us to make the mistake of judging one another when we unconsciously assume that everyone started out with the same knowledge base as ourselves, which is unrealistic. We all were brought up differently; our parents may have had different values, different beliefs and different views, and even their educational as well as ethnic background would have played a part in our upbringing. So it is easy to see how we could be very wrong in our lifestyles, thinking, feelings, judgments and many other aspects of our lives. Just as every appliance you purchase comes with a user manual, so do you.

Can you remember what it was like to put an item

together avoiding referencing the user's manual, only to find that the item is not constructed correctly, you may even find parts left over that you know belong in the construction, your only option now, Is the user's manual.

Believe it or not, this is how we live our lives every day, and because humans are a lot more complex than an electrical appliance, by the time we realize we've made a mistake, the effects can be long-lasting and devastating, and although the user's manual can help at this point, we all know how painful and time consuming rework can be. It's obvious that up until now, most of you have never had anyone to show you GOD's purpose for us, and how important it is to our well being, mentally, physically, and spiritually, if you think about it, these are the three areas in life where people suffer.

GOD holds each and every one of us responsible for knowing what we are supposed to be doing. If you have loved one's suffering, sick or dying, or you yourself are suffering sick or dying, you and they can have peace, and if that means nothing to you, think of your loved ones whom have already passed on, isn't there someone you would like to see again, Grandparents, Mother, Father, Sister, Brother, Son, Daughter etc. Make an effort to know; because come judgment day when you're before GOD, "I didn't know" won't be acceptable, the door will be closed to you.

Enjoy the book!

CHAPTER ONE

THE SEXES

This chapter explores the nature of the male and female existence as it relates to dating, mating, and social interactions, and gives a brief illustration of the differences between the two and their struggles to exist in union, as well as the challenges they will face in their pursuit of love and happiness.

1

Men and women are totally opposite beings. Men
are very simple by nature, and are often driven by
physical and visual assessments, where as women
are more inclined to use mental and emotional
perceptions before an assessment, the two are about
as opposite as they can possibly be. This is why the
Union of a man and a woman is so complex. Men
on an average are very easily attracted by sight, and
will form a complete opinion, right or wrong, about
whatever he sees. If a female is attractive and
appears to be decent, he will assume she's OK,
without ever having held a conversation with her.
Women, on the other hand, whom can be attracted
by sight, tend to be more selective and inquisitive
before forming a final opinion. The sexuality of the
two basically follows that same scenario. A man
can become intimately stimulated within seconds
after seeing an attractive women; initially his
emotions play no part in this attraction, his feelings
seem to develop somewhere in between intimacy
and the relationship afterwards. Women, being
more the intellect of an intimate relationship,
usually aren't easily stimulated intimately simply by
sight. Often much mental and emotional stimulation
is required before a woman's physical stimulation
catches up to that of her counterpart, "THE MAN".
As a rule, women usually require a sincere interest,

some form of affection and appreciation, only then, does physical stimulation come into effect. This is where it gets tricky, so now, let the games begin! The man's objectivity becomes primarily to satisfy his intimate desires, as the woman's objective becomes one to achieve a lifelong partner. Both feeling they have something to protect begin a sort of courtship tug of war which can sometimes last throughout an entire relationship. This tug of war between the two exists primarily due to a woman's need to protect her emotions, reputation and future, while men attempt to protect their freedom of commitment which supports promiscuity, allowing them the opportunity to choose and experience as many women as they may find themselves attracted to. In fact, in an attempt to keep their sexual appetites satisfied, men will often play up to whatever a woman wants, and as they become acquainted, the transformation begins. Both morphing into whom they believe their expected to be, oppose to who they really are. For example, the ultimate goal for most men is usually one of sex, where-as women, unlike men, have their own goals, which rarely involves sex. Women on the average are looking for a commitment. They are well aware of men's relentless desire for sex, and will give in just enough to excite this relentless desire. Once a woman sees his obsession with it, she knows she is in control. This obsession with sex can leave men vulnerable, allowing women the opportunity to manipulate them almost indefinitely; however, this sort of manipulation does have its consequences, which usually result in some sort of secret resentment towards women by men. Most men will allow themselves to be manipulated in exchange for sex, due to their obsession. They know they are obsessed, but are unwilling to change. This is where the manipulation is reversed on the woman, also known as (flipping the script).

This is a slang terminology that means reversing the situation; which derived out of the film and movie industry. So now, if or when a man succeeds in seducing a woman, whom he holds resentment towards, he will lose interest in her almost immediately, and begin to treat her like an enemy conquered, oppose to a beautiful intimate encounter. Sensing the negative treatment and distant attitude, a woman will begin to feel somewhat used and unappreciated, which is the exact opposite of what a woman needs most. This "of course" cause women to develop a resentful attitude towards men, and the two will go on that way repeating this cycle of misery until they mature or separate. The relationship between men and women has always been this way; it hasn't changed much since the beginning of time. If we look back in history we will find in stories like Adam and Eve: (Genesis 3:2-19) Samson and Delilah (Judges 14:12-18)

4

David and Bathsheba (2 Samuel 11:2- 17) that a woman's basic nature is one of restlessness, envy, glorification, and insatiateness. The characteristic of men are pride, dominance, glorification, and an overwhelming fixation on sex. But of course there are exceptions to the rule; however, we will be focusing on the rule (the majority). Sex is used in almost every situation you can think of. People will use sex to pay debts, earn money, pass time, etc, and it's not just individuals, but society as a whole. As a matter of fact, our societies (especially its leaders) promote degenerative behavior, its principals and policies as it relates to sexual matters are some of the most immoral unnatural course of conducts ever taken. You would expect adults to be experienced enough in sexual matters to have a higher degree of moral standards.

Men, unarguably have been the leaders of this society, and are therefore primarily responsible for its ruin, but women are by no means innocent in the matter. If we take a look at all of the sexually immoral contributions women have made in this society, we will find that women have been very diligent in their rolls. For instance, there could never be a pornographic Magazine, or any other pornographic materials that are geared towards men, without the consent of woman. Women are also responsible for the demand and sales of sexually suggestive clothing, which they are more than eager to wear. This encourages young girls to wear them, and follow that same path of irresponsible degenerative behavior.

Women whom succumb to this kind of behavior are the leading cause of sexual promiscuity among men women and children, they are also among highest percentage of women whom have dysfunctional relationships with men, and remain to be the leading contractors of STD's. One of the primary ways women contribute to the promiscuity of men is through sexually suggestive clothing. When men see women dressed sexually provocative, they have the tendency to fantasize, which often leads to actions. You may ask, how is this the woman's fault? Well let me say, "I'm glad you asked" Men (on the average) have a very high level of sexual hormones, compounded with an over-active imagination. They (as a rule) seem to have a higher sex drive than women, reasons' being unknown, but what we do know is that women are well aware of this fixation of men, and seem to get some sort of ego boost out of manipulating them because of it. We also know that in the beginning, God blessed both man and woman with the act of sex to populating the earth, which stands to reason that it must also be he whom is responsible for the high level of sexual hormones and pleasure that comes from it which causes men to be so fixated with it: (Genesis 1:26-28). But men are by no means excused from this degenerative behavior; they are responsible for their actions and shall be held accountable. This is why Solomon, (a man of God) "gave subtlety to the simple and knowledge and discretion to young men" instructing them in the course of conduct to be taken when interacting with immoral and unrighteous women:

Proverbs 6: (KJV)

23 For the commandment *is* a lamp; and the law *is* light; and reproofs of instruction *are* the way of life: **24** To keep thee from the evil woman, from the flattery of the tongue of a strange woman. **25** Lust not after her beauty in thine heart; neither let her take thee with her eyelids. **26** For by means of a whorish woman *a man is brought* to a piece of bread: and the adulteress will hunt for the precious life. **27** Can a man take fire in his bosom, and his clothes not be burned? **28** Can one go upon hot coals, and his feet not be burned?

So as you can see, this immoral unrighteous behavior of women goes way back to biblical times, but notice the kind of women that it speaks of (Evil, Whorish, Adulteress) this would be all of the (tight and explicit clothes wearing, twerking, sexually suggestive) females who participates in such acts, young and old! But men with sexual addictions are spiritually and morally rebellious, who have taught themselves to be weak, which renders them powerless, and empowers their source for sex, (women) whom definitely enjoy controlling them. Women whom enjoy this kind of power fail to realize that it's a false power, and that they are only as powerful as the man is weak, and once he satisfies his need for sex, their power diminishes. This explains why men after having sex, lose interest in the woman, and have no desire to be close or affectionate, which leaves woman feeling confused. His only interest was in her ability to satisfy him sexually, and once this has been accomplished, he has no further need for her, until next time. This creates frustration in a relationship, because neither person are getting what they really need, and blame each other. But it isn't just men whom suffer from vulnerability, women have a vulnerable side themselves, which renders them powerless and empowers men. Both could spare themselves much disappointment and unhappiness if they would resist the temptation to control one another through the weaknesses in ones character. Women appear to be cursed with a weakness that is so destructive, that once they become addicted it's nearly impossible to recover. It is (the need for attention) women have such an enormous need for attention that they themselves are vulnerable. This is the power that men have over woman, and men have become very proficient in the use of this power. Every woman likes to think she is somehow, prettier, smarter, sexier, more exciting, better, etc, than the next.

That's what makes a man's objective so achievable. As weak as men are sexually, so are women emotionally. If women would spend some time validating their own self-worth, irrespective of what any other woman has, says or does, it would greatly diminish a men's power over them. Men and women are naturally attracted to one another; we've proven this earlier as being established by God, as he stated to the first man and woman on earth "BE FRUITFUL AND MULTIPLY "encouraging them to become intimate and reproduce.

This makes it the natural order of things, but mankind (of course) always finds a way screw things up. Mankind (men and women) have taken blessings such as love, romance and intimacy to its lowest level. This lack of appreciation for such blessings are perpetuated from one generation to the next, instilling the wrong principles and values in the youth. Young boys are taught to lust instead of love, while young girls are encouraged to seek affection through sexual suggestions. So almost all of us start out in the wrong frame of mind, and this is why so many people develop terrible sexual

9

habits and desires. In its natural form (untainted) sex is a beautiful experience, capable of nourishing emotional deficiencies that are essential for a healthy personality and character. There's an old saying that goes: (when a woman is being bitchy, she lacks sexual gratification) this saying evolved out of the many studies that show how sexual activity can lower the anxiety and stress level of an individual significantly. And I'm sure that if you've ever experienced sexuality, this needs no pointing out, although a woman being bitchy is likely to be more complex than sexual gratification. Sex alone has no spiritual or emotional nurturing, it's just a physical act of the flesh, but when love is involved then it becomes nurturing, emotionally and spiritually, gratifying, which is what it's all about, that is why we fall in love, get married, have children etc. Make no mistake about it; women are extremely emotional and delicate, very much like a flower, beautiful to look at and sensitive to the touch, but just like a flower, if it is too cold that can kill it, if it is too hot that will dry it out, her spirit must have just the right amount of nurturing, requiring constant care. In fact, a woman's emotions can soar from elation to despair in a matter of seconds for no apparent reason what so ever, it's a mood swing that's often uncontrollable, and it's the female hormones that dictate this erratic change in nature. Men however, usually maintain some level of consistency when it comes to emotions, and once they become focused, it takes a very dynamic situation to interrupt their intended course. This characteristic of men is partially to blame for the lack of performance in the bedroom, it isn't that men aren't capable, but rather that they are so fixated with the end results that lack of attention is given to emotions. It is also why men are capable of achieving orgasms much faster than women, which almost always results in the dissatisfaction of women. It's easy to see how this can become a problem when you consider the fact that women are emotional, and emotions are a major part of a woman's Character, especially during intimacy. Unlike men, whom do not require an emotional connection during intimacy, women do, and are usually very appreciative of passionate communication during intimacy. Women also require a significant amount of time to process information during intimacy than do men, which is why there is such a discrepancy in the timeframe that each will experience an orgasm.

This unique characteristic of the two constantly raises questions about each other's ability to perform. Women will bash men charging that they can't sustain an erection, and men charging women with the inability to have an orgasm, when really they both are somewhat misunderstood. Let's go back to the beginning to reveal some of the issues

surrounding our misunderstanding of one another.
From the time a young girl starts to develop an
interest in boys, she is taught to restrain herself
sexually, and this is good. However, young boys are
taught just the opposite, and in fact are encouraged
to express sexual attraction, but not in those exact
words, it's more subtle.
Their introduction to sexuality comes in the form of
subliminally driven messages which are usually
filled with good intentions, but does lack accurate
and appropriate information.
This misinformation is often taught by older males,
such as friends or siblings that may have had some
form of intimate interaction with the opposite sex
that could be construed as experience, although
parents have been known to dish out some bad
advice of their own. Often time's young girls will
express feelings of interest long before young boys
are ready to return these feelings. Young boys are
usually content grouping together, challenging one
another, competing and impressing each other.
They're quite capable of entertaining themselves for
hours without any intervention from girls, and in
fact, they even implemented a rule that would
prohibit girls from participating. It was called the
(No Girls Allowed) rule. They would enforce this
rule whenever they grouped together, building
clubhouses, going camping, taking on adventures
and etc, and would ban any boy caught associating

with a girl. But of course as the teen years approach, everything changes, especially with a little persuasion from the girls. Boys at this age become very interested in girls, and once a young boy develops an interest in girls "WATCH OUT", its full speed ahead. If a parent doesn't have control at this point, they may just as well forget it, because there's very little reasoning with a teenager smitten with the opposite sex. The attraction that young boys and girls have for one another is extremely normal, but it's a very new and powerful experience, and should be closely monitored with adult supervision. Attraction, love, and romance are very subtle emotions that pack a big punch, and teenagers aren't capable of handling everything that comes with it, in fact (most adults aren't). This vast arena of emotions can be challenging to a relationship, and the weaker of the two will be the most vulnerable, and he or she is in for the ride on their life. Usually it's the women who experience this hellish ride due to the fact that women are typically caring and attentive, thriving on affection and attention, and at times will do almost anything for that attention. One of the biggest mistakes women make in this most sought after attention is their dress ethics. They believe dressing immoral is the way to be noticed, thinking it will get them the attention they crave, but what they don't realize is that the attention they crave isn't the attention they'll

13

be getting. Even when they become wise to this fact it appears to have no affect on the way they conduct themselves, their only concern becomes the need for attention, any attention! Men see this as an opportunity for sexual promiscuity, and what's really interesting, is that women who carry on this way seem surprised to discover that the only thing men want from them is sex, (imagine that).

So the man begins his relentless pursuit of sex, encouraged by the woman's immoral and inappropriate attire, and if she's attracted to him she may give in to his advances to retain him in hope of a relationship, but everyone knows you can't build a relationship based on sex, it requires much more. Besides, relationships based on sex never work because the intimate needs of women will vary, as well as men, and what may be pleasing today may not be as desirable tomorrow, or it may be days, and even weeks before a woman needs any intimate attention at all. This characteristic is more noticeable in older women, but as for younger women, they tend to have a sexual appetite equal to that of men, which is one of the reasons older men are attracted to younger women, so due to the fact that men have a higher libido than women, they are more equally matched in a relationship with a younger woman, which promises more frequent intimate encounters. Another reason older men are attracted to younger women is because they're

14

usually less exposed, which causes them to be more enthusiastic and excited about the experience, as well as physically sound. Most men prefer women who have retained as much of their virginal qualities as possible, which is why it is very sound advice to abstain from sex until after marriage, because this allows both individuals to share the experience from the same standpoint, which will result in a better experience for them both, and a longer lasting love life, and it's morally correct as well. If a woman maintains herself virginally, size wouldn't matter. Women usually become size sensitive when the form of their physical structure begins to diminish, and lose its natural characteristic. This can be caused by childbirth, to many partners, or lack of self maintenance; and even experiencing sexual activity at an early age can contribute to the loss of a woman's physical structure. But for those women who have turned their lives around but can't quite get their bodies to agree, size may just be a real issue, and in such cases a woman may do well to be in a relationship (preferably married) to a man who's physically a cut above the norm, especially due to the fact that women who have maintained their original physical structure typically find it too unpleasant of an experience to interact with such men, especially considering that men during intimacy tend to be very liberal in their delivery, and no woman enjoys

15

being pushed beyond that which is normal, "there certainly isn't any pleasure in that". Even men whom are a cut below the norm are very capable of performing very well intimately, and have no physical limitations what so ever, and are in fact obviously very capable of impregnating women, even those of whom who have not retained much of their original virginal qualities, or whose natural form and physical structure has diminished. Furthermore, intimate gratification has never come from the size of one's genitals, "as a matter of fact", pleasure is generated by the actions of the individuals' involved (preferably married), and everything else which is necessary for the enjoyment of intimacy already exists between the two sexes. The evidence of this fact is masturbation, which has been around for many years.

Many people have used this practice for many reasons, which may range from lack of a mate to avoiding promiscuity, STDs, pregnancy and even commitments, but whatever the reason, it isn't a very healthy alternative to intimacy (marriage), and many things can take place during this act that will put it in the category of immorality and unrighteousness, or even perversion, such as:

1) How often are you doing this?

2) Where is it taking place?

16

3) What is your mental status? (Perverted/or pure)

4) Is there a real need for it?

And those are just a few of the many questions that will need to be addressed because masturbation can be a very inappropriate and unhealthy practice. For example, during masturbation individuals often fantasize, and if such is the case, than whom are you fantasizing about? If it's anyone other than your spouse, then you're lusting, and that's a sin. Or maybe you're just visualizing using sexually suggestive material, or some other medium, which is all really pornography, and that's a sin. But one of the more disturbing drawbacks to such a practice is its ability to destroy your natural affection for the opposite sex, which will cause you to lust instead love, and slowly diminish your desire for love, while increasing your need for self-satisfaction. So now when you do become intimate, you will be insufficient, because your objective has become self-gratification, which causes all kinds of relationship woes. That alone can make the relationship between men and women very awkward, causing men to subconsciously view women as sex objects, totally disregarding their mental and emotional needs. Masturbation can also be a very powerful practice, with very negative and addicting consequences, so it would be best to avoid such a practice altogether. We should keep in mind that sex is a form of expression, and its purpose is to share intimate affections with someone of the opposite sex with whom you have a committed relationship, (preferably married), and to bear children. It isn't a competition, nor was it ever meant to be the finale to a night out on the town, or something people do in casual passing. It's a very sacred act, and when expressed sincerely, any female of age is compatible with any male of age, and there's nothing magical or mysterious about it. Also keep in mind that pornographic materials are very damaging to the morals of individuals, especially the youth, as it depict inappropriate acts between men and women, and often in a very unnatural demeanor while portraying women as loving it," sadly" many women accept that sort of treatment believing that this is how it's supposed to be, enduring pain, disrespect and abuse and calling it love, but what the materials fail to show are the millions of people who are damaged by this behavior, mentally and physically.

Another destroyer of lives and relationships is "LUST" this is the monster of monsters when it comes to sexual morality. This act can do so much damage to the mind that you may never be the same again. It's a silent destroyer of sexual morality, and has a cancer like affect with the characteristics of carbon monoxide and gas, which means that once you realize you've been affected, the damage is already done. It's so subtle and learned at such an early age that recognizing it is almost impossible. It has led many astray, destroying minds and lives. And here's how it works; basically, you brainwash yourself to believe whatever you want to believe when you lust, and the object of your lust doesn't have to do anything because you will do it all. Now just imagine if the person you're lusting after wanted to manipulate you, there would be very little effort required on their part because you will have done most of the self-manipulation on your own, and now there would be two brains working against you, "yours and theirs" and yours would be the most damaging because it holds all of the information about you: your weaknesses and strengths as well as your needs desires and fantasies, very vital information which will assist in the manipulation of your principals and morals. Millions of people do this to themselves everyday, which is known as "blowing your own mind". And this is how it works; you lust for someone so hard that you make him or her out to be more than they really are, basically manipulating yourself. Lust can be very effective in the practice of self manipulation. If a manipulative person has lust working in their favor on your behalf, they could literally control you. Lusting can also be very offensive to someone who does not welcome that sort of attention, especially if you're a stranger. However, men aren't as easily offended by this kind of behavior, but of course men have a much lower moral standard than women.

But decent woman will almost always take offense to such behavior, "remember" women can be very temperamental, but there are times when they themselves aren't as bothered by such behavior, and will sometimes even appear to enjoy it, but those times are usually few and far between. Lust is responsible for the birth of many children, as well as unwanted pregnancies, adoption and abortions. Often the two people involved in this equated lust have no intentions of being in a committed relationship or becoming parents, which further victimizes the children whom are born out of this act of selfishness, and exposes them to years of neglect. This is a problem that may never go away because people detach themselves from the consequences of their actions when lusting, this is all made possible because lusting allows you to think only of yourself. Lust is also responsible for many unions, such as courtship and marriage, but these unions often have a very low success rate, as to be expected. And when you consider the fact that the only thing keeping two people together is lust, it's easy to understand why so many relationships end in disaster. No relationship worth preserving can survive on lust, but people will actually build

20

relationships based on that, fully aware of their incompatibility, and because they fear losing each other, they refuse to admit that theirs is one built on lust.

So they continue living a lie as things get worse, and eventually the relationship is unsalvageable, and the very thing that brought them together (Lust) loses its appeal. Lust also encourages a person to lower their standards in their quest of a lifelong mate.

If lust is the method by which you gauge the success of your relationship, it's destined for failure because lust is a temporary emotion. This means that once you've satisfied your lust, the mood subsides leaving you face to face with reality, questioning the validity of your interest, and even though more sincere feelings may develop in the future, it's impossible to make a life changing decision such as marriage or children while under the influence of lust; this is why it is so important to remove lust from the equation. But there are women who find it flattering to have men lust for them, because it gives them a false sense of being special, and they will even encourage this lustful behavior by dressing provocative. Most women have not yet learned that lust has no boundaries, and is an act of selfishness with no promises of commitment and allegiance, or loyalty. If a person lusts for one they'll lust for all, and the reasons don't matter, the fact is, there will always be someone who has what you have, more or less. None of us are more special than the next where lust is concerned. So "ladies" if lust is what attracts a man to you, "beware" because once a man has used you like a public toilet, he will move on to the next, regardless of how beautiful or well structured you think you are. And men "beware" because if lust is what attracts a woman to you, then you're in for a ride as well, because once a woman has manipulated and secured her status with you, she'll move to the next shiny lure in the pond just as she did with you, regardless of how well polished you thought you were. Lust is also the root cause of infidelity in many relationships, which we all know has lead to many breakups and divorces, and in even worse cases, death. It may seem as though lust is harmless, but it's much like a drug, which means the more you do it the more you'll want it, and the more you want it, the more addicting it becomes. This is where fornication and adultery comes into play because the more you lust, the greater the desire, which compels you to act, but in the process of acting people get hurt, and lives are destroyed, all because of something that seemed so harmless.

God has given us authority and control over our minds and bodies, so if we allow things to spin out of control, "THAT'S OUR FAULT" and there's nothing more for him to do, and we will be responsible for our actions. God created sex for male and female as an act of intimacy and bearing children, and anything outside of that is the perversion of mankind. "Sex" is what it is, and not what you'd like it to be, so if you have other sexual ideologies, then there's a day of judgment for that, and you'll have to answer to God!

CHAPTER TWO

MORALITY

This chapter exposes the nature of
immorality in men and women, and
clarifies many misunderstandings and
myths associated with the two, as it
establishes the truth in morality with a
knowledge and wisdom greater than
the knowledge and wisdom of
mankind.

As stated in the introduction, we were all raised with someone's views and values on life, which is our first experience and exposure to morality/immorality (**right and wrong - good and evil**).

No one whom has ever lived has had the knowledge of right and wrong or good and evil at birth. Nor were we born predestined to be firemen, policemen, teachers, politicians, singers, dancers etc, but instead, we come into this world destined to be only one of two things, and that is "**Male** or **Female**" everything else has to be taught. Even (**heterosexuality**) as well as (**homosexuality**) has to be taught, but we're defiantly not born with a knowledge base to know either, and there isn't anything in our DNA or brain matter that predetermines our sexual preference or attractions, and those who promote such doctrine, only do so out of ignorance or deception.

So for us to get a clear understanding, we will need to go back to the beginning, back to biblical times. Not many people are aware that there's a war going on in this world, which is "**good** versus **evil**" (**God versus Satan**).

All of the issues that exist in the world today where there's a conflict with mankind in matters of (**right or wrong / good and evil**) only exist as sub-issues. The bigger picture is (**God versus Satan**).

25

Look at it this way: in the same manner that
computers have main folders and sub folders, we as
humans have that same structure with a higher
power.

God and Satan are the higher powers that represent
two separate (**MAIN FOLDERS**),

God (**the good folder**) and Satan (**the evil folder**),
and every man woman and child on this earth is a
(**SUB-FOLDER**).

So your existence in this world as a **Sub-folder**
primarily depends on which **main-folder** you fall
under. But remember, in the computer world, Sub-
folders cannot share separate main-folders, they
may only exist under one Main-Folder.

This same rule applies with God; you're either a
Sub-folder for God or a **Sub-folder** for Satan.

This is what Jesus was speaking of when he says
that "**you cannot serve two masters**", his point is
that there will be conflict, and you will be disloyal
to one or both of them:

Matthew 6:24 (KJV)

24 No man can serve two masters: for either he will
hate the one, and love the other; or else he will hold
to the one, and despise the other. Ye cannot serve
God and mammon.

We have all been given a **free will** to choose. And
any physical action that requires thought and

decision to create movement, has to be chosen; and only you have the power to will these choices of your body. This is what is known as **free will**. In other words, no one can take thought and have you to raise your arm, or take thought and have you stand from a seated position. These actions all have to be summoned by you!

This is especially true as it relates to sexuality, which requires much more thought and decision to create an action.

Everything we do in life starts from a thought, and we have the ability to either nurture or reject those thoughts. This is where your upbringing will play a very important role as to which "**Main Folder**" you will fall under.

If you were raised with Biblical values and you choose to accept them, then you will use that platform in your decision making throughout life. On the other hand, if you were raised with worldly values, then you will most likely use that platform in your decision making in life.

What are worldly values?

Worldly values are values that are pretty much the opposite of Biblical values, and some worldly values can be very deceptive as they start out on a Biblical note but then take a turn about mid stride and become tailored to fit each person's individual desires.

In fact, the largest part of the population on earth uses worldly values, and many people that were raised with Biblical values will shed them for worldly values to achieve some desired goal that would otherwise be unacceptable by Biblical standards. So when someone says that *"they were born this way"* **(Gay or Lesbian),** we know with great certainty that this is a lie, and that these individuals are refusing to accept responsibility for their actions, in which society supports. Unfortunately, this is a society that will allow excuses as a scapegoat in finding individuals not guilty of their faults and crimes, but fortunately for the world there are still those whom will not excuse unacceptable behavior, and do hold those whom are responsible accountable. Even God himself speaks out against **(Gay and Lesbian)** lifestyles through his word the Bible, and God would never allow us to be born as something that is beyond our control, and then deem it **(UNGODLY)**. This would be a law against his own self and against his own works, because it is he who created and established the process that procreates **male** and **female**. He would have to punish himself first. So once again the excuse: **"I was born this way"** won't work with God or true Christians alike. Besides, God is very clear in his establishment of mankind, as he created only two genders, **(male and female)** and nothing in between:

Genesis 1:27 (KJV)

27 So God created man in his *own* image, in the image of God created he him; male and female created he them.

Genesis 2 (KJV)

7 And the LORD God formed man *of* the dust of the ground, and breathed into his nostrils the breath of life; and man became a living soul.
21 And the LORD God caused a deep sleep to fall upon Adam, and he slept: and he took one of his ribs, and closed up the flesh instead thereof;
22 And the rib, which the LORD God had taken from man, made he a woman, and brought her unto the man. **23** And Adam said, This *is* now bone of my bones, and flesh of my flesh: she shall be called Woman, because she was taken out of Man.

Everything that God has established, Satan sets out to destroy, and this is why (Gay and Lesbian) lifestyles exist today. Gays and lesbians have been around since ancient times, this isn't anything new, in fact, throughout history they have been removed or forbidden from society for many generations, but every so often in the passing of time as society spirals out of control, removing God from the equation, it allows for this behavior to resurface to epic proportions, like what we see today. But if you follow biblical teachings, it strongly suggests that this generation and maybe even the next could very well be the final chapter in this world's back and forth struggle of good versus evil.

There is definitely a struggle in this world between **good** and **evil**, (**God verses Satan**).

Satan destroys lives, while God seeks to save them. So everything that God establishes, Satan counters to destroy, like a game of chess or checkers, but the stakes are (you and I).

So God has established Holy matrimony between **man** and **woman**, and instructs that no man should put this union asunder. And he's speaking of the union between **male** and **female**.

And the word (**asunder)** means: (**to do away with, separate, or take apart**). He further instructs that this is the reason that a man should leave his father and mother, that he may take a wife.

Matthew 19:4-6 (KJV)

4 And he answered and said unto them, Have ye not read, that he which made *them* at the beginning made them male and female,

5 And said, For this cause shall a man leave father and mother, and shall cleave to his wife: and they twain shall be one flesh?

30

6 Wherefore they are no more twain, but one flesh. What therefore God hath joined together, let not man put asunder.

This speaks clearly to the union of **male** and **female**, and it is very clear of God's intentions, stating that **"no man"** is to do away with this arrangement, **NO MAN**! This means (**mankind**) which includes **male** and **female**. So if you are of flesh and bone, and blood flows through your veins, then that means you! In fact, God has made it so that even animals are aware of this arrangement, unless of course, "they live with you" But in spite of the facts, there are some who like to make the argument that there are some animals that practice homosexual behavior, which is absolutely false, but for the sake of argument, let's play devil's advocate for moment…let's say that you are able to find a species or two that does display this kind of behavior, it still proves absolutely nothing in the way of support f or Homosexuality, because these would be animals, which are far from the intelligence capacity of humans, so if they were to aspire to such behavior, **"they're beasts"** (**not humans!**). Besides, animals are kept in check by nature and humans' by (**morality**). Furthermore, even in documentaries where you may witness a single incidence of a pack animal (*always a young male*) mistakenly attempt such an act, they're

31

quickly put in check by the rest of the pack, which is not to be construed as the entire species experimenting with homosexuality, because even the youth have to be taught, which you will learn later in chapter three.

And we know that this wasn't God's intentions when he told Noah to build an ark, and to collect a **male** and **female** of every creature and put them in the ark to preserve life, he certainly didn't do it to destroy all that was bad in the present world so that they could go and start a new one of Homosexuals:

Genesis 6:19 (KJV)

And of every living thing of all flesh, two of every *sort* shalt thou bring into the ark, to keep *them* alive with thee; they shall be male and female.

So God has established the (**Heterosexual**) lifestyle, and Satan counters with a (**Homosexual**) one, in an attempt to destroy what God has established by influencing millions, "both **male** and **female**" to put asunder that which God has established. Satan knows that to destroy mankind and defeat God, he must work through mankind to get it done, he cannot just arbitrarily raise his hands and destroy the entire world, because God will not allow it, but God does allow Satan free rein throughout the world for a period of time as they battle for the souls of mankind.

But make no mistake about it, God is the more powerful of the two, but because Satan has challenged God, stating that people will only love him and serve him for a reward, so God has given Satan a certain amount of time to prove his claim, and God is set to prove that those whom really love him will do so out of love, even during hard times and much suffering. And God isn't speaking of those whom claim to be Christians, or those whom will forsake him and take whatever road is easiest during hard times, he is speaking of those whom are just the opposite.

This is why so many people cannot stand the test of time, because once you've chosen God, he chooses you, which means that the trials and tribulations will be many, and very lengthy, but bearable. The length of this time just depends on God, no one else knows. You may have heard about the Biblical story of a man named **"Job"** (pronounced Jobe), who faced this same scenario:

Job 1: (KJV)

1 There was a man in the land of Uz, whose name *was* Job; and that man was perfect and upright, and one that feared God, and eschewed evil.

6 ¶Now there was a day when the sons of God came to present themselves before the LORD, and Satan came also among them. 7 And the LORD said

33

unto Satan, Whence comest thou? Then Satan answered the LORD, and said, From going to and fro in the earth, and from walking up and down in it. **8** And the LORD said unto Satan, Hast thou considered my servant Job, that *there is* none like him in the earth, a perfect and an upright man, one that feareth God, and escheweth evil? **9** Then Satan answered the LORD, and said, Doth Job fear God for nought? **10** Hast not thou made an hedge about him, and about his house, and about all that he hath on every side? thou hast blessed the work of his hands, and his substance is increased in the land. **11** But put forth thine hand now, and touch all that he hath, and he will curse thee to thy face. **12** And the LORD said unto Satan, Behold, all that he hath *is* in thy power; only upon himself put not forth thine hand. So Satan went forth from the presence of the LORD.

The point of the story is that he was tested in his love for God; you really must read the whole story to appreciate the great love that this man had for God, **"it's an awesome story"**.
And we aren't any different, we must also do what is right and **"eschew"** (abstain from) evil just like Job. But it can be tough sometimes to know just what to do, being that this society does its best to

remove God from all of its teachings, and misleads so many to acts of immorality.

The leaders of society know that if they can remove God from their teachings, then they can control mankind and take the place of God. They know that the bible holds the truth, and that the truth will set you free. Free of their **lies**, **control** and **perversions**. So they concoct stories of mankind's beginnings and existence to deflect any and all belief in God.

They know that if they can get you to denounce the Bible, then they'll have full control. They will even go as far as to have you believe that mankind's existence started from apes, or that billions of years ago, a molecular cloud gave birth to mankind and that we are star children. It just goes on and on. But when you think about it, what else would they say, after all, keep in mind that these are people who want to take the place of God, and decide for their selves what is right or wrong. Think of it this way, what do most people do when they want to remove someone and take their place? They will defame that individual with lies, deceit and any other method of defamation to achieve their goal. Some will even resort to assassination to succeed. Just look at the Candidacy process of running for any level of office in this world, it involves so much defamation that the people lose interest. And it's no different with men wanting to replace God, whom will say whatever it takes to remove God and take his place, whether it's in their own lives or the lives of others. This is exactly what Satan is all about, "removing God and taking his place". Satan is very cleaver, and plays a major role in getting people to believe in the defamation of God, or that there's no God at all. There are many people who follow this concept, which are commonly known as (**Atheist**). An atheist's point of view is that men can govern themselves and each other, and that there is no need for a higher power to lord over mankind.

But we see everyday how that's working out…."right?"

On the other hand, people that are Christian minded believe that there is a higher power as lord, and that mankind needs to be led by a single minded view that's for all of mankind and not just selective views. Christian minded individual **(truly Christian minded)**, and not your typical imposters, believe that morality is not their call but God's, and that everyone is subjected to it, and no one's exempt. But in all of the societies in this world, God is omitted and men lord over men; which is why we have (***lies, deceit, perversions, murder, favoritism, greed, hatred, anger, sickness, disease and so on***). This is an everyday acceptance in the world, and even considered the norm by almost all.

But everything in the bible teaches against all of these things, *"now having said that, I shouldn't have to write any further"* because you would think that everyone wants a life free of those things. However, mankind is continually evil, if there is a right way and a wrong way; men will choose the wrong way almost every time. You're probably thinking.... how did we get this way? Well the answer is simple: It's a learned behavior that has been passed down for thousands of generations. "You must remember" there aren't any thoughts or behavior that relates to social interactions that hasn't already been done by those before us. We are not the first people on the planet. These struggles in life have always existed; they're only new to us.

One of the behaviors that have been passed down for thousands of generations is the (**Gay and Lesbian lifestyle**) "so once again" you are not the first "**Gay or Lesbian**".

And if you are honest with yourself and take a look back, you will find that you were in no ways born that way. There had to be some incident in your past that lead to this behavior.

It is a proven fact that the early stages of our lives are the most impressionable ones, as we are at a place in our lives where most of our foundation will be established.

"Even the most agnostic of the so-called specialist couldn't disagree with this"

But as we get older we become more stubborn, resistant and defiant. Just take a look at yourself for example, how willing are you to search out the truth, to change, or even just listen.
Are you: *Stubborn, resistant and defiant?*
This is why children are recruited at such an early age in life for sports, academics, competitions and many other areas where success requires a great focus and commitment to succeed, because in the early years there's less (**stubbornness, resistance and defiance**), which makes the goal more achievable. Now don't misunderstand, I'm not saying that children are sought out at an early age by society to insure that there will be a (**Gay and Lesbian**) community, because I don't believe that's the case at all. The point I'm making is that you may think you were born Gay or Lesbian because you were exposed to it at such an early age when there was less resistance, and you had not yet had a chance to build a good moral foundation.
That is why it is so important to train children in righteousness and morality at an early age; you need to fill their minds with thoughts of morality continually. Morality should be the core value of their thought process; this will prevent society from influencing their thoughts with immorality and

perversions. Children that are raised with true biblical values will always hold to them throughout life, and even if they become distracted or make mistakes, they will always revert back to their teachings.

Proverbs 22:6 (KJV)
6 Train up a child in the way he should go: and when he is old, he will not depart from it.

You may have heard people say "there's nothing wrong with being Gay or Lesbian" but these people are actually blaspheming against God. Anyone that claims to be a Christian or who acts as if they are accepting of God but speaks in support of, or are accepting to the Gay and Lesbian lifestyle isn't a true Christian at all. If God says that something is wrong, and you say that it isn't, then you are speaking against God. You are calling God a liar. You are taking the same position as Satan; he denies everything that God says. You have made yourself an enemy of God's and an ally of Satan's. This goes back to not having two masters. Jesus walked the earth teaching this very thing, and many people rejected these teachings and went against him, making themselves anti-Jesus. But Jesus was teaching the word of God which is Christianity, and he became known as Jesus Christ, and to follow him and his teachings was known as being "*Christ like*"

39

and those who were against him were known as anti-Christ. There are many *antichrists*. Are you an antichrist?

Do you support teachings or doctrines that are in opposition to what Jesus taught? If so, then you are an **(antichrist)**. Even atheists are antichrists.........

1 John 2:22 (KJV)
22 Who is a liar but he that denieth that Jesus is the Christ? He is antichrist, that denieth the Father and the Son.

So you can see by the biblical definition given above, even you may be an "**Antichrist**".
There are presidents, senators, congressmen, governors, mayors, councilmen and many others in an office of leadership and authority that support teachings that are *antichrist*. They support teachings that deny that Jesus is of God and is righteous and true. You cannot say that: "**you support Gays and Lesbians**" or that "**there's nothing wrong with being Gay or Lesbian**" and be a Christian or (of Christ), because those are (*antichrist*) statements. Some will even attempt to shield their immoral behavior by stating that it is wrong for us to judge one another, which is really ironic coming from an antichrist mindset considering that (**us not judging one another**) is a

Biblical passage. However, there's a big difference between judging and informing. If you are informative to others based on Biblical laws and values, this isn't judgmental, but informative. It's only judgmental when you form opinions based on your own views and values. Furthermore, we are instructed by **"God himself"** to teach one another against improper and immoral behavior. So not only should someone be telling you about your improper and immoral behavior, but you too should be telling others about theirs. This isn't being judgmental at all, it's being obedient. Jesus clearly states that we (everyone) are suppose to teach one another biblical values, and not support or encourage improper or immoral behavior:

Matthew 5:19 (KJV)

19 Whosoever therefore shall break one of these least commandments, and shall teach men so, he shall be called the least in the kingdom of heaven: but whosoever shall do and teach *them*, the same shall be called great in the kingdom of heaven.

Many people will construe this as being judgmental, which is why it is so important that in your efforts to inform others of immorality, you do not act as if you are God, because you are not God, but are as puny and flawed as everyone else in his eyes. So

41

when you're correcting others, "remember" you are
only delivering a message (**being informative**).
And even though it would be nice to save a soul or
two, it really isn't your place, because even at best,
you are only a messenger, not "**Moses the
deliverer**". And this goes double for "**preachers,
pastors, clergymen, reverends, bishops, popes**"
and anyone else who seem to think that they are of
some great status with God.

Now having said that, let's take a look at what Jesus
has to say about it, because I know that some will
be offended, and attempt to distort the truth with
rhetoric, but Jesus (again) clearly states that the
only way to God is through him "**period!**" No one
else is privy to this. Not "**preachers, pastors,
clergymen, reverends, bishops, popes**" or any
others that will make such a claim, let's take a look:

John 14: (KJV)

5 Thomas saith unto him, Lord, we know not
whither thou goest; and how can we know the
way? 6 Jesus saith unto him, I am the way, the
truth, and the life: no man cometh unto the Father,
but by me.

So Thomas was asking Jesus, how will they know
what to do once Jesus was gone, and Jesus stated: "**I
am the way, the truth, and the life: no man
cometh unto the Father, but by me**" so Jesus was

instructing them to follow his teachings only, **"not others"**, because no one else is **"the way, the truth, and the life"**.

Now don't misunderstand, anyone can pray with you or for you, but no one's prayers to God is received by God as more esteemed or as priority over another's, (and once again) that means no **"preacher, pastor, clergymen, reverend, bishop, pope"** or any others.

We are all heard equally by God when we pray, so **"no one"** and I do mean (**NO ONE!**) takes priority.........

Romans 2:11 (KJV)

11 For there is no respect of persons with God.

Proverbs 15:29 (KJV)

29 The LORD is far from the wicked: but he heareth the prayer of the righteous.

So it doesn't matter who you are, as long as you are seeking righteousness, then God will hear your prayers. But on the other hand, those whom are unrighteous, prayers aren't heard, regardless of their titles and status, or how esteemed they may think they are. So if you have chosen to live unrighteous, then **"God is far from you"** just as the verse above describes.

Many people think that because they belong to
churches, or world ministries and organizations,
they have established themselves with God, but we
know this isn't true by the verses given above,
which state that "**you must live righteously**" and
not wickedly, you cannot have two faces: (**one for
God and the other for Satan**). Remember what we
learned earlier: you cannot serve two masters.

Those that live this way seem to think that they are
saved in Christ, but there will be a rude awakening
on that day of reckoning, as Christ will reject many,
and even go as far as to say:
"I never knew you"

Matthew 7: (KJV)

21 Not every one that saith unto me, Lord, Lord,
shall enter into the kingdom of heaven; but he that
doeth the will of my Father which is in heaven.
22 Many will say to me in that day, Lord, Lord,
have we not prophesied in thy name? and in thy
name have cast out devils? and in thy name done
many wonderful works?
23 And then will I profess unto them, I never knew
you: depart from me, ye that work iniquity.

"Don't let this be you!" Don't be as the atheists, or
as those of the world who think that there will be no

judgment. In fact, let me share with you a conversation that I once had with an individual whom was bordering atheism, or probably more of an agnostic but teetering towards God. We were into an in-depth conversation about righteousness and God, and in conclusion he summed it up this way, stating:

"The bible teaches that living a healthy clean and pure life can prevent many pitfalls and be very enjoyable as well. So you don't lose anything to do so. Besides, if you live according to God's will and find in the end that God isn't real, there's really no harm done, and you don't lose anything. But if you live your life according to the world, and find out in the end that God is real, then that would be a catastrophe" because you lose everything!!

So where you are in life isn't nearly as important as where you need to be, just as your choice to be Gay or Lesbian isn't as important as your choice in being free, but society has hidden the truth which has left many of you deceived, by removing the word of God out of everything. For example, men were created by God and did not evolve from apes, and were given the opposite sex to love, not to be Gay and Lesbian mates. To cultivate the earth (a masculine task) given to man, but seeing him alone God decided wasn't a good plan, because even the animals had partners, which were of the opposite sex, so God gave man a partner, and the name (Eve) describes her best. But partners in today's societies have taken another aim; it refers to (Gays and Lesbians) which Satan proudly claims. But God created heterosexuals while homosexuals are Satan's joy, because everything that God has established, Satan sets out to destroy, but the establishment of God which now pertains to man, follows this scenario and will forever stand: man was created for God and the woman was created for man, with Christ as the head of them both to carry out God's plan. Many people have chosen Satan just as the Gays and Lesbians have done, and society supports their decision and encourages everyone, which is something to be expected of a society full of sin, whose number one agenda has become the feminization of men.

But believe it or not, there were always Gays and Lesbians, even in biblical times. The Gay men of those times were called (**Sodomites**), and displayed all of the behavior that Gay men of today do, despite the fact that there were biblical teachings against the feminization of men. They were taught that men were not to wear anything that was designed for a woman, or act in anyways feminine.

46

This is why we know that this current system of the
world is not ran by men and women of God,
because their teachings support all of these things in
which God "**not only considers a sin**", but an
(**abomination**), such as the <u>Gay and Lesbian</u>
lifestyle, which is a whole different level of sin.
And for those who aren't aware....an (**abomination**)
is something that is so wrong that it's (**unthinkable,
inconceivable**), and a total (**disgrace**), against
"**God and nature**", "and that's just a mild
definition". It's just the same as cursing God to his
face, because you're mocking his establishment of
the male and female relationship, "**which really
pleases <u>Satan</u> well**". And even though we all
commit sins every day, most sins are natural, which
isn't to say that it makes them OK, because they
aren't any more acceptable to God, "*not by any
stretch of the imagination*", but they're usually
(**moral acts**) that are committed in an (**immoral**)
setting, or they may be acts that start out natural and
are then pushed to the extreme, and therefore
become (**immoral**).

For instance, the following is an example of a
(**moral act**) committed in an immoral setting:
<u>fornication</u>, we all know that the act of sex itself
isn't a bad thing, it's a "**natural act**", but if it is
performed between (**unmarried individuals**) then
that setting makes it a bad thing, "**a sin**!"

Another example is: **drinking**, which is a natural
act, permissible by biblical standards, so there's
absolutely nothing wrong with having an alcoholic
beverage, but too often it's pushed to the extreme,
and individuals become drunk or alcoholics, so it
becomes a bad thing….an act that started out
natural but got pushed to the extreme, "**a sin!**".
So in essence, there are many acts which are natural
for us to do, but when taken out of context they can
quickly become "**sin**".
However, the act of (**Homosexuality**), starts out an
"**abomination**" and ends an "**abomination**", a
(**sin!**), and has no place in **Christianity**, **God**, or
Nature, and "in fact" goes directly against God and
nature, and there's no situation or circumstance on
earth where it's appropriate.
And men have always cared for one another, such
as friends, relatives' associates' etc, It's a very
natural thing in relationships, but once it becomes
intimate in nature, then it becomes unnatural, (**an
abomination**). Most Gays and Lesbians insist that
the Gay and Lesbian lifestyle isn't sexually driven,
but to the contrary, "that's exactly what it is". Gay
and Lesbian relationships are strictly of a sexual
nature. Sex is actually the driving force in these
relationships, otherwise they would just be friends
that cared for one another with no intimate
attractions what so ever, this kind of relationship
exist between (**heterosexuals**) all the time, but to

48

become intimately attracted is where it becomes a
sin. It refers back to "**a natural act being pushed
too far!**"

Even if you find that you prefer the company of
those whom are of the same sex more than those of
the opposite, it should never be construed into
anything more than brotherly or sisterly love. And if
"*for whatever reason*" you find that you aren't
romantically attracted to those of the opposite sex, it
isn't the end of the world, and your life doesn't have
to end because of it, as there are many people
whose lives are very fulfilling having chosen a
lifestyle of abstinence. But abstinence requires
much self control and discipline, regardless of the
subject matter, which may prove to be an epic task
for an individual who is Gay or Lesbian due to the
fact that such a lifestyle is of a "**sexual nature**", as
is "**fornication**" and "**adultery**".

But people will often defend these acts with sayings
like (***I'm only human***) or (**don't judge me**) and
even (**God isn't finished with me yet**), which of
course is to be expected, because everyone has an
excuse, "however", an excuse should only be the
reason why you may have become a certain way,
but it should never be the reason why you remain
that way. In fact, every excuse that you can possibly
think of has an expiration date, and it's usually just
about the time that everyone is as tired of hearing it
as you are of using it. And we're not talking about

49

legitimate facts that would actually prohibit you from a course of action, but an excuse which is used as reasoning for your lack of control of a situation, as if it were out of your control, when in reality it isn't. But **"facts are facts"** and are undeniable, they will flat-out confirm or deny an excuse, and there's no two ways about it.

For example: being born (**Black, White, Asian, Jewish, Latino**) and so on, is a circumstance in which you have no control, and the fact is, you can't do anything about it, but being compelled to be (**Gay or Lesbian**), simply isn't a fact, but an excuse.

Another example of things that are out of your control, which is a fact: is that you cannot leap off of a building and fly, nor can you command the sun to rise or set, or start and stop the rain. These are all acts in which you have no control, which is a fact, but to say **"you have no choice"** as to how you will live your life, is a flat-out excuse!

And as for men and this whole femininity act, this is something totally different than just being Gay, because men who put on the facade of acting like women, only do so out of **"female envy"**, which is to say that these men envy women so much, that they fall into the character of a woman. It's just what any actor or actress does when getting into character for a roll, and we know this to be true because men can be gay without the feminine facade, just as a man can be feminine without truly being gay. Besides, just think of the effort it takes to transform yourself into something you're not, it requires much effort and planning on your part, which really isn't convenient at all, and even though there are many who don't seem to mind, it isn't nearly as convenient as being yourself.

So when you look at it in its entirety, there seems to be more deception and confusion going on than anything, in fact, so many People have been lied to and manipulated into these lifestyles, that even they don't know what's right anymore, but either way, it's up to us as adults to do the right thing. You can't continue blaming others for your choices; you must stand up and take responsibility. Just admit, that you prefer **immorality** over **morality**, and that you reject God's establishment of (**male and female**) relationships, for Satan's alternative (**Gay and Lesbian**). Admit that you believe you know better than God what is **good** and what is **bad**, because that's exactly what you're doing.

You may not have known these things because no one is speaking the truth, which has been cleverly designed for them to take advantage of you, but you're also to blame for not knowing what to do, so much of your ignorance is really self-induced.

But this book wasn't written to tell you what to do, I'm not a priest, preacher or pastor so I won't lecture you, but what it does intend is to break through the facade, by giving you the facts, not of men but according to God, because we live in a society that has no shame, which even takes pride in perversion called change, so they disregard God to make up their own rules, which satisfies Satan and even most of you, and now it's time to make choice as they are faced with the dilemma, and they've decided that the truth doesn't fit their agenda:

"Homosexuality"

But truly righteous individuals will always except and embrace correction; they will not become offended, confrontational, or even driven to the point of strife because of correction. And although it may lead to a few hurt feelings initially, it wouldn't amount to much more than ruffled feathers.

This was the demeanor that Jesus had; he was not argumentative or confrontational. He was always approachable and willing to engage in conversation, but never scornful.

You will see many people today very scornful in their treatment towards one another, even when discussing the bible, which clearly teaches against such behavior, but they still carry on this way.

The bottom line is: "**you are responsible for your actions**", which is why you should be looking into the right and wrong of a matter, and not let anyone dictate to you. And while it's ok to hear what others have to say, you should always check things out. Don't accept anyone's word as Gospel, except that which is according to the bible. This is why I will give you biblical chapters and verses throughout this book as a point of reference for everything that I say, and I will do my best not to throw an abundance of them at you at one time, but some of it will be necessary for you to check it out for yourself. And I (strongly!) recommend that you use the (**KJV**) "**King James Version**" as a point of reference, and the reason being, is that you need to receive the most **accurate**, **un-tampered** version of God's word as possible, so that you may receive as much of the truth as possible, and the "**King James Version**" is just that!

It was published over 400 years ago back in *1611*, and is the most accurate account of God's word than any bible ever written or printed after it, even unto this day, especially when it comes to keeping the original **content**, **context** and **emphasis** in its teachings. This is especially important because the bible has been re-written and published many times over in different versions, and much of the original text has been changed, and when you change words you compromise the message, and the intensity of the message as well as the intentions of a message.

For example: look at the message below, and then notice the two different translations of it.

Original message: Tell Roy **"to come home now and clean his room or he will be sorry"**.

Translations:

1) Roy, mom said **(to come home and clean your room)**.

2) Roy, mom said **(if you don't come home right this minute and clean your dirty room, you are going to wish that you had)**.

So even though both translations deliver the point of the message, to: **(come home and clean the room)** Example (1) is a little laid back and doesn't emphasize the seriousness in which this needs to be done.
And example (2) is a bit excessive and over exaggerates the message.

So as you can see, changing the meaning of a message is a very serious thing, especially if you are saying that someone said something that they didn't say. But some would argue that it isn't that big of a deal, when in reality, it is, and here's why....every message has an intended purpose, and usually it's informative, but most often it's to get someone to respond, or to do something, and that's when the delivery is important. But if you alter the message, it may not have the intended punch to incite the recipient, or you may portray the wrong demeanor of those sending the message, which could cause resentment from the recipient towards the sender, and that would be counterproductive for the intended purpose of the message. And of course there are times when it won't matter as much, but then there are times it could be a matter of life or death.

So it's very important to be accurate in your delivery.

And your delivery should always be as accurate as possible when referencing God. This will prevent misinterpretations which can cause others to stumble, or lose interest and shy away.

In fact, those who misrepresent God, and claim to speak in his name, saying that he said things which he did not say, have no Idea of the **"Hell"** they'll have to pay, especially those who claim to be ordained in God's name:

Jeremiah 23: (KJV)

1 Woe be unto the **pastors** that destroy and scatter the sheep of my pasture! saith the LORD.
2 Therefore thus saith the LORD God of Israel against the pastors that feed my people; Ye have

scattered my flock, and driven them away, and have not visited them: behold, I will visit upon you the evil of your doings, saith the LORD.

Deuteronomy 18:20 (KJV)

20 But the **prophet**, which shall presume to speak a word in my name, which I have not commanded him to speak, or that shall speak in the name of other gods, even that prophet shall die.

I Timothy 3: (KJV)

*2 A **bishop** then must be blameless, the husband of one wife, vigilant, sober, of good behaviour, given to hospitality, apt to teach;*

8 Likewise must the **deacons** be grave, not doubletongued, not given to much wine, not greedy of filthy lucre; 9 Holding the mystery of the faith in a pure conscience. 10 And let these also first be proved; then let them use the office of a deacon, being found blameless.

So as you can see, it's a very serious matter to God, that those who represent him are **righteous**, **just**, and **true** "Blameless", which is why the verse

above expresses that those who choose to do so,
must be **"proven first!"**
Never the less, people of the world seem to think it's
cute to use these titles, but have no idea of the
seriousness of them, or the consequences for the
vanity in which they are used, but as you can see,
God takes it quite serious, and *"understandably so"*
especially when you consider that it is the
misappropriation of these titles, and the truth behind
them that has led to so many different
interpretations of God's word, which has ultimately
sparked the many denominations that exist today,
and is even responsible for the many lies which
have contributed to millions of people choosing to
live (**Gay and Lesbian**) lifestyles every day.
Even the government's hands are full of blood, as it
leads millions to slaughter with its legislation of this
behavior. Isn't it ironic that this same government's
currency states (**In God We Trust**), and it's the
same government that chants "**God Bless
America**", have you ever seen such hypocrisy?
The only people who should be supporting the Gay
and Lesbian agenda are those who openly and
consciously reject God. So if you confess that God
isn't real, or that he is real but you declined to
accept him, then you have openly and consciously
chosen to reject God, and therefore accept your fate.
All others should be upholding righteousness,
which doesn't mean Gay bashing, because that sort

57

of behavior is equally unacceptable to God, whom does not except one unrighteous behavior over another. But what God does expect, is the continued education of his word, with the same love and patience for one another that he has shown us since the beginning of time.

However, love and patience doesn't mean to become acceptable to inappropriate behavior, God definitely isn't in support of that, but he does want us to reject inappropriate behavior, but it's to be done with love, and not hate.

So even though Gay and Lesbian lifestyles are condemned by God, whom instructs us to reject such behavior, there will still be those that charge you with being "**Homophobic**" for obeying God's word, but what they call **homophobic**, Jesus calls **righteousness**, and that's what really matters.

This is one issue that isn't up for debate, there is absolutely no reason to get into foolish debates with anyone whose opinion differ. If it is God that you serve, then it is his laws in which you must abide. But those whom live by man's laws of immorality obviously do not accept God, which is why there isn't room for debate. "**God's laws do not change**", they are the same **yesterday**, **today**, and **forever**, but as for mankind, their laws change continually, to suit whoever's in charge.

But currently, there's a shift in nature taking place which is driven by God, and is causing Satan to be more desperate than ever, and he isn't leaving any stones unturned, and will not go down without a fight, which is why his influence exists in every facet of life, especially within the degenerative behavior of men, who have become more feminized today than ever before in the entire history of men, even to the point of being more needy than "women and children".

Men are even adopting the roles of women, in **relationships**, the **work place**, and even as **leaders** of society. They have even created a custom in culture termed (**Metro sexual**). And for those that aren't familiar, this is basically a man that pays way too much attention to himself, much like a woman would, such as: (**makeup, coloring of hair, nails, jewelry**) and so on.

The bible calls this behavior in a man: (**effeminate**) and condemns it.

Men have even become more feminine in demeanor, and have become more dependent on women than women are of men, especially when it comes to **relationships** and **break-ups**.

Now days when a woman breaks-up with a man, it is he who does the whimpering and whining, stalking and complaining, and will even resort to murder because his feelings got hurt, totally in despair, "**void of all masculinity**", stoically depleted!

Even the (**stay at home dad**), which is the epitome
of an oxymoron, is a shame to his children. And
even if you weren't biblically educated, or trained in
the structure of a man's role in life, nature itself
provides all sorts of examples for you to observe.
For instance, did it ever occur to you why the
woman was chosen to give birth, or why she's the
one designed for breast feeding? And has it ever
even crossed your mind that there's a purpose
behind the process of a woman's menstrual cycle?
These are all feminine qualities in which a man will
never possess.

Women were strategically designed to raise
children, to be their first point of contact and
communicator to the world. This is the natural order
of things for all living creatures.

But the feminization of men continues to contribute
to the decline of mankind in all civilizations. The
masculine mindset is rare, and even when found it's
usually distorted due to a lack of biblical
knowledge. One of the more noticeable shifts in
society where men have crossed over into women's
rolls is the office place, there are way too many men
sitting at desks these days, even hosting/co-hosting
gossip, **exploitation**, and **frivolous** talk shows. And
it isn't that women are limited to these kinds of
rolls, but due to their nature and demeanor, they're
more natural in them, and therefore do a much
better job than men!

There has been a total decline in the male character over the years, which leaves young boys hard pressed in finding good positive masculine role models, even in their own fathers. We are now living in a society that embraces the feminization of men in all of its teachings, such as teaching boys to show affection to one another as if they were females, and encouraging men to be less stoic and more temperamental.

This shift in nature has become more dynamic over the past decade or so due to the infiltration of feminine men into leadership roles of society.

It's like the old saying, (**a chain is only as strong as its weakest link**) in other words, it doesn't matter how strong all of the other links are, because if just one link is weak then the chain won't hold, so they all may as well be weak.

In the case of society, all of the weak links are in the leadership roles, so **decisions**, **views**, and **legislation** will all be geared towards that weak mind set, and in this case it's feminization, which applies to every aspect of life.

For example, if you have a person that's a (**raciest**), and that person becomes a police officer, then you will have a (**raciest police**), or if you have a person that's a (**pedophile**), and that person becomes a priest, then you'll have a (**pedophile priest**), and so on, and the same is true with the leaders of society, which means that since you have (**feminine**) men as leaders, the agenda then becomes (**the feminization of men**). And that's all it takes for the degeneration of a nation, where millions are led to slaughter by just a few. But ultimately, it's your responsible to know right from wrong, and the parents are responsible for the children until they are grown to choose on their own, and after that, the entire decision making process will be theirs, and theirs alone.

So how do we know what's right? "**Common sense**" which suggests that there has to be a gauge, or some sort of guide that's used to govern our behavior, and determine our actions. So how do we find it, and where do we even began to look? There are many questions like these that have yet to be addressed, but do you really think that man has the answers, and if so, then where did he get them, who told him what is good and what's bad? Certainly mankind isn't this great oracle of knowledge and wisdom in matters of good and evil.

We know by history that man has always been immoral by nature; this has been proven in every generation of every society. And every governing body of society has always evolved into immorality and corruption, which "*no one can dispute* ", in fact, there are numerous accounts and documentation of immorality and corruption in every governing establishment of society since the beginning of time. And believe it or not, even heaven has had its share of immoral behavior, which erupted into war. As a matter of fact, it was in heaven where it all began, because Satan **"like many of you"** became rebellious and was therefore ejected from heaven to earth, and has been allowed to reign over it ever since. He's actually the primary inspiration for all **evil**, **wickedness**, and **immorality** which people have chosen throughout history, even unto this very day, as shown below:

Revelation 12: (KJV)

7 And there was war in heaven: Michael and his angels fought against the dragon; and the dragon fought and his angels, 8 And prevailed not; neither was their place found any more in heaven. 9 And the great dragon was cast out, that old serpent, called the Devil, and Satan, which deceiveth the whole world: he was cast out into the earth, and his angels were cast out with him.

12 Therefore rejoice, ye heavens, and ye that dwell in them. Woe to the inhabiters of the earth and of the sea! for the devil is come down unto you, having great wrath, because he knoweth that he hath but a short time.

So you can see that Satan's time on earth **"is short"**, so he knows he's finished, but he wants to take as many of you with him as possible, because for him

63

that would be a victory against God. So his whole purpose is to **"deceive as many of you as possible"** and show God that people will choose him over God, which is why the bible describes those who serve Satan, **"as his children"** because they are against everything that God has established, spewing one lie after another, even to the point of denying that God even exists. They will even tell you that the bible isn't real, but after all, this is exactly what Satan does. So isn't it conceivable that a <u>**father**</u> would teach his <u>**children**</u> as he himself does?

Let's take a look.........

John 8: (KJV)

44 Ye are of your father the devil, and the lusts of your father ye will do. He was a murderer from the beginning, and abode not in the truth, because there is no truth in him. When he speaketh a lie, he speaketh of his own: for he is a liar, and the father of it.

So you see here, that not only is **"The Devil a Liar"** but *"the father of it"*, he invented it!
You must remember that the only way their lies can stand is to deny God. They have to try and convince you that God doesn't exist, otherwise, they would have to admit that God's word is true, and that he is

the authority on righteousness, "*not man!*" But this would discredit their excuses, and force them to face the truth, even if they choose not to accept it. But whether you accept it or not, the only way we can possibly know righteousness, is by way of God. If God did not make it possible for us to have his word (**The Bible**) we would be lost in man's twisted way of thinking. We wouldn't have any way of searching out the truth in man's teachings, and would therefore be subjected to society's ideology of what is right and what is wrong.

So even though people may refuse to use it, God has given us an awesome tool in (**The Bible**), and with it, we can challenge any authority or situation, and prove it to be a **lie** or the **truth**, and that's what they don't like, they being: "*the leaders of society*" (Satan's children).

I like to think of the Bible as (**a manual for humans**), and like an appliance that you would purchase from a store comes with a manual, "so do we", and it's as important in knowing our functions as manual for an appliance.

How many times have you tried to install or assemble a product without using the manual, only to make a mess of things, then you have to go back with the manual and try to correct it, providing you haven't caused permanent damage. Imagine that same scenario with your life, you could really ruin it. So why not do it right the first time; study the

manual (**The Bible**) before you ruin the product
(**You**).

And never let anyone dictate to you righteousness,
make sure that it's consistent with the Bible,
because no one is an authority on righteousness,
"*No One!*" in fact, We're all a mess in some way or
another, which is one of the reasons why God made
sure that we have his word.

But don't be like some people who get discouraged
or panic because praying and seeking God seems to
be to no avail, remember, God does hear your
prayers, and he knows your needs even before you
ask, as Jesus describes:

Matthew 6: (KJV)

7 But when ye pray, use not vain repetitions, as the
heathen do: for they think that they shall be heard
for their much speaking. 8 Be not ye therefore like
unto them: for your Father knoweth what things ye
have need of, before ye ask him.

And of course you know he sees all, so it's not like
he isn't there, but he has given us the bible for a
reason, and believe it or not, most people's
problems are self inflicted, and it's because they're
not using that "**manual for humans**" (**The Bible**).

Here's an example:

let's say that someone leaves you in charge of their home while they're away, and they instruct you to use a tablet that they've left behind which has in it everything that you will need to manage while they're away, but whenever a situation arise, you're constantly calling them asking what to do, and all the while, the solution to your problems lies in that tablet that they've left behind, but you simply refuse to use it.

Now here's a breakdown of this example below:

- **Earth is the home** - and the home owner that is away - is (**God**)
- The person left in charge while the home owner is away - is (**Us**)
- The tablet left behind which you simply refuse to use - is (**The Bible**)
- The constant calls to the home owner asking what to do - is (**Your prayers**)

This is exactly what we do with God every single day. We continue to ask him for answers which he has already provided in the Bible, "*so you will never get a response!*"
Now don't misunderstand, "you should pray", but it's the type of prayers that you've been praying that may be questionable.

For example:

1) You will hear many people say that they are seeking God for a mate (**husband or wife**), but instead of asking God to help you find a mate, why don't you use his word (**The Bible**), and the parameters set there-in to do so. After all, God isn't a matchmaker. And only once in the history of this world has God ever brought two people together, and that was (**Adam and Eve**).
The choice of coupling is a liberty that he gives to you, so use it.

2) And instead of praying that your **spouse**, **children** or **family members** have some sort of miraculous intervention from God that will cause them to live righteously, why don't you set some real life boundaries "**again using biblical principles**" and hold firm to them, while requiring that those around you do the same, this would be more realistic and beneficial.

The alternatives given above is what the Bible is all about, and is a more realistic approach to happiness than to pray that God forces someone against their will to please you. "Now of course" you can pray for whatever you like, but you should be realistic in your prayers, because some prayers just aren't going to be answered, and here's why:

God has given us the ability to do many things, and often times, we will pray to God asking him to do something that he has already done, or has made it possible for us to do, so to pray a prayer like this, "is a wasted prayer"

Here's an example:

Let's say that you're home alone sitting in the living room hungry, but there's plenty to eat in the kitchen, and your prayer is that someone will come home and prepare something for you to eat, **"wouldn't you say that, that was a wasted prayer?"**
But this is what we do every day. We pray for things that are with-in our power to do, and then become disappointed because our prayers aren't being answered.
But on the other hand, some prayers aren't answered because **"we do not put God first"**, or because we put **friends** and **family** before God, but Jesus is very clear on this matter:

Matthew 10: (KJV)
37 He that loveth father or mother more than me is not worthy of me: and he that loveth son or daughter more than me is not worthy of me.

So knowing this, why would you ever put what someone else says above what Jesus says?
Such as: the (**Gay and Lesbian**) lifestyle, your mindset should be.....who cares what anyone wants if it doesn't comply with what God wants, and since no man comes to God except by way of Jesus, "I really don't think" that you want to put your **friends** or **family members** before Jesus, and put yourself in a position of being "**unworthy**", because of their mess!
But when you make statements such as "**it's ok to be Gay or Lesbian**" or "**Gays and Lesbians are born that way**", or even accepting the (**Gay and Lesbian**) lifestyle by condoning this behavior and allowing it in your presence, then you put yourself in a position of being "**unworthy**" of Jesus, and are therefore "**unacceptable to God**", which is a prime example of loving **friends** and **family** "more than God".
Jesus explains that when you choose God (**righteousness**) you "**will**" lose friends and family, because not everyone is willing to give up sin for righteousness, "**including you!**" which is why you continue to except your **friends** and **family** immoral behavior. But God isn't like the leaders of society; he doesn't allow escape clauses in his laws, because if you are in any way accepting or supportive of such behavior, (*even if you yourself do not participate*) you are still guilty "**period**". The only

70

escape clause that God allows is called
(**repentance**).

This is what Jesus was speaking of when he said
that he did not come to earth to bring peace, but
instead he is bringing a sword, and that he has also
come to set variances among mankind.

This means that you will have to make the "**tough
choice**" of losing **friends** and **family**, because when
you choose righteousness over sin, it will set family
members and friends against you:

Matthew 10: (KJV)

34 Think not that I am come to send peace on
earth: I came not to send peace, but a sword. 35 For
I am come to set a man at variance against his
father, and the daughter against her mother, and
the daughter in law against her mother in law.
36 And a man's foes shall be they of his own
household.

Now for those of you with little understanding, this
doesn't mean that Jesus came to earth to start
trouble and disrupt families, it's just his cleaver way
of saying that when you choose to follow him,
(**righteousness**), it will cause **family members**,
friend, **coworkers**, **acquaintances** and all others to
stand against you, because they themselves have not
chosen to do so. This is all a part of that cross that

Jesus was speaking of when he says that **"whoever doesn't take their cross"**, isn't worthy of him.............

Matthew 10: (KJV)
38 And he that taketh not his cross, and followeth after me, is not worthy of me.

You may or may not be familiar with the cross that he is speaking of, but Jesus died on a cross for all of mankind, but before he died he was torched by People that were against truth and justice, (**much like many of you**), and your leaders of society today, which is the majority of the people in the world. This is why there's so much evil and unrighteousness in our societies: <u>government</u>, <u>churches</u>, <u>schools</u>, **"and even your own home!"** But during this torture he was nailed to a cross, which was two pieces of wood fastened together to look like a lower case letter T (t), then erected vertically and fastened to the ground with him on it, and they continued to ridicule and torture him until ultimately crucifying him.

So when Jesus says **"he that taketh not his cross, and followeth after me, is not worthy of me"** it's a metaphor, which signifies that you will encounter opposition and resistance in the name of Jesus and righteousness. So the terms: (**take your**

72

cross) or (**bear your cross**) simply means to endure
the consequences (**trials and tribulations**) that
comes with accepting God in a world that hates
him, "**even unto death if necessary**".
And everyone has a cross, "that's right!" anyone
who has ever walked this earth, have had or has a
(**cross to bear**), which is why Jesus says "**he that
taketh not his cross**" and didn't say (**he that
doesn't choose a cross**).
So even though Jesus literally suffered and died on
the cross, he is speaking metaphorically when he
says "**he that taketh not his cross**". The cross is a
metaphor for the trials and tribulations that you will
have to endure due to your choice in righteousness.
And there are times when the trials and tribulations
will closely resemble being nailed to the cross, due
to the fact that those who are against righteousness
will ridicule and try you, just as they did with Jesus,
and maybe even unto death. But whatever the case,
you must bear the cross to be worthy of Jesus,
which really shouldn't be a problem because if the
unrighteous are willing to die for unrighteousness,
then the righteous should definitely be willing to die
for righteousness.
So even though everyone has a cross to bear, not
everyone's cross consists of the same issues.

For example:

You may have an issue with **drinking or smoking**,
where as someone else's issue is with **drugs**, and

another's is with **fornication**, and so
on........**adultery, idolatry; pornography,
corruption, lying, cheating, stealing, pedophilia,**
or **homosexuality**, and many other immoral and
inappropriate acts that are self destructive
degenerative behavior, "which are too many to
name"

These are all cross bearing acts that are to be
resisted by those whom are tempted, in which you
must take up the fight of righteousness against
Satan's attacks.
Satan is the (**author of the lie**) and the (**inventor of
evil things**), he is the source of all of your immoral
and unnatural behavior, because it is he who
inspires these thoughts. There was once an old
saying many years ago that went: **"the devil made
me do it"**, it was very funny and entertaining, but in
all seriousness, Satan **"can't make you do
anything"** {**GOD FORBIDS!**} and it is by God's
own law that he doesn't allow Satan to force anyone
against their will, just as God himself will not force
you against your will, but he does "however" allow
Satan to tempt you, so that you may prove yourself
to be **worthy** or **unworthy**, just as he did with the
example of Job, a righteous man of biblical times.

Let's take a look:

74

Job 1: (KJV)

6 Now there was a day when the sons of God came to present themselves before the LORD, and Satan came also among them. 7 And the LORD said unto Satan, Whence comest thou? Then Satan answered the LORD, and said, From going to and fro in the earth, and from walking up and down in it. 8 And the LORD said unto Satan, Hast thou considered my servant Job, that there is none like him in the earth, a perfect and an upright man, one that feareth God, and escheweth evil? 9 Then Satan answered the LORD, and said, Doth Job fear God for nought? 10 Hast not thou made an hedge about him, and about his house, and about all that he hath on every side? thou hast blessed the work of his hands, and his substance is increased in the land. 11 But put forth thine hand now, and touch all that he hath, and he will curse thee to thy face. 12 And the LORD said unto Satan, Behold, all that he hath is in thy power; only upon himself put not forth thine hand. So Satan went forth from the presence of the LORD.

So God did allow Satan to try Job, and there's actually much more to this story, and in the end Job proves that he loves God despite all of Satan's accusations that he only loved God for the Blessings. It's a very interesting story, but you'll have to read the rest of it for yourself, I just wanted to point out that God does allow Satan to tempt and try you, which allows you the free will to choose **righteousness** or **unrighteousness**. And sometimes the temptation will be with great fear tactics, and other times it may be as simple as a subliminal suggestion, but either way, you are totally free of will to accept or reject it, just as you are with being **(Gay or Lesbian)**.

Here's another example of Satan trying to tempt someone to do something, but in this example, it's Jesus:

Luke 4: (KJV)

3 And the devil said unto him, If thou be the Son of God, command this stone that it be made bread. 4 And Jesus answered him, saying, It is written, That man shall not live by bread alone, but by every word of God. 5 And the devil, taking him up into an high mountain, shewed unto him all the kingdoms of the world in a moment of time. 6 And the devil said unto him, All this power will I give thee, and the glory of them: for that is delivered unto me; and to whomsoever I will I give it. 7 If thou therefore wilt worship me, all shall be thine. 8 And Jesus answered and said unto him, Get thee behind me, Satan: for it is written, Thou shalt

worship the Lord thy God, and him only shalt thou serve. 9 And he brought him to Jerusalem, and set him on a pinnacle of the temple, and said unto him, If thou be the Son of God, cast thyself down from hence: 10 For it is written, He shall give his angels charge over thee, to keep thee: 11 And in their hands they shall bear thee up, lest at any time thou dash thy foot against a stone. 12 And Jesus answering said unto him, It is said, Thou shalt not tempt the Lord thy God. 13 And when the devil had ended all the temptation, he departed from him for a season.

So even Jesus whom was perfect and true was approached by Satan to be tempted, but in Jesus' case, he was approached with riches and glory, where as Job was approached with pain and suffering, but in both cases they resisted being tempted by Satan, and remained true to God. Satan is constantly seeking out those whom he can influence against God, just as he did in Jesus' case, but when Satan couldn't tempt him, it says that **"he departed from him for a season"**. So Satan is never done with you, he knows all of your weaknesses and exactly when to attack, which means that you need to be alert at all times, you cannot afford to be morally impaired, which is another good reason not to drink alcoholic beverages, since they have a definite propensity to impair judgment.

And it's an indisputable fact that countless numbers of people have lost their lives, and have even taken the lives of others while under the influence of alcohol and drugs, and believe it or not, it's a mentally altered state which is prime territory for Satan to operate, and being the master of deception, he is very influential in getting you to believe whatever it is he wants you to believe. So it's of the utmost importance to remain vigilant and sober at all times...........

I Peter 5: (KJV)

8 Be sober, be vigilant; because your adversary the devil, as a roaring lion, walketh about, seeking whom he may devour:

And you must be extremely careful of those whom claim to represent Christ or God, because Satan cleverly uses these individuals to hide behind God's name, since he knows that it's pure and righteous, and will cause you to drop your guard. He knows that if he can get you to believe that these individual come in God's name, then they will appear more believable, and even he himself will appear as an angel to deceive you:

II Corinthians 11: (KJV)

13 For such are false apostles, deceitful workers, transforming themselves into the apostles of Christ. 14 And no marvel; for Satan himself is transformed into an angel of light. 15 Therefore it is no great thing if his ministers also be transformed as the ministers of righteousness; whose end shall be according to their works.

Remember, (1Peter 5:8) warns that Satan comes as a **"roaring lion"**, which means that he's showing no mercy, and is coming at you with everything that he's got, and just as (2 Corinthians 11) above describes, it shouldn't surprise you that all of the **(preachers, pastors, clergymen, popes, reverends, apostles, bishops, deacons, evangelists)** and others who claim to preach or teach on God's behalf, are false, and are instead workers of Satan! You must also remember what we learned earlier, that Satan tries to destroy all of God's works, and he has made a great push with the **(Gay and Lesbian)** agenda, but it is God that will destroy all of Satan's works, **"which includes you!"** if you're a part of Satan's work:

I John 3: (KJV)

7 Little children, let no man deceive you: he that doeth righteousness is righteous, even as he is righteous. 8 He that committeth sin is of the devil;

for the devil sinneth from the beginning. For this purpose the Son of God was manifested, that he might destroy the works of the devil.

So (1John 3) above, describes who is righteous and who belongs to Satan (**the Devil**), and it's very clear. *" Read it again if you need to!*" But it's very easy to see whose piece of work you are, which is why we need the Bible. The Bible is the only true source of righteousness that exists for reproving and correcting ourselves, and each other:

II Timothy 3: (KJV)
16 All scripture is given by inspiration of God, and is profitable for doctrine, for reproof, for correction, for instruction in righteousness: **17** That the man of God may be perfect, thoroughly furnished unto all good works.

So now you know that the Bible (**Scripture**) is inspired by God for our instructions and correcting ourselves, but to have good success, we must train ourselves in the proper way of thinking, because everything we do will be affected by our thinking. Earlier we learned that many thoughts will come to mind through the power of suggestion, but it is up to us to except or reject them. That is why it's so critical that your thoughts are aligned properly, which can only be done through training.

And here's how it works:

If you allow yourself to think improperly, then all of your reasoning and understanding will follow that same pattern, and before you know it, you aren't able to discern between right and wrong. You will even try to find reasoning in unrighteousness. This is what the bible describes as **"Reprobate"**. You will become **"reprobate minded"**, which means that your thought process will be void of righteousness; even your decision making will literally become a matter of whatever pleases or pleasures you at that time, **"total immorality"**. This is mostly what we see in the world today, which is why there's so much support and acceptance of immoral behavior, it's also the reason that a person can be (**Gay or Lesbian**) and never see the immorality in it, because it's all due to a **"reprobate mind"**.

"And once again" this behavior was displayed in biblical times as well, and because people did not want to keep God in their thoughts, **"much like today"** removing God from **schools**, **businesses**, **homes**, God chose to remove himself from the people, and left them with the inability to access him or his knowledge:

Romans 1: (KJV)

28 And even as they did not like to retain God in their knowledge, God gave them over to a reprobate mind, to do those things which are not convenient; 29 Being filled with all unrighteousness, fornication, wickedness, covetousness, maliciousness; full of envy, murder, debate, deceit, malignity; whisperers, 30 Backbiters, haters of God, despiteful, proud, boasters, inventors of evil things, disobedient to parents, 31 Without understanding, covenantbreakers, without natural affection, implacable, unmerciful: 32 Who knowing the judgment of God, that they which commit such things are worthy of death, not only do the same, but have pleasure in them that do them.

Notice the term **"haters of God"** that word (**haters**) was used even in biblical times, and I'll bet you probably thought it was something that this generation brought about, but there's an old saying that goes: **"history only repeats itself"** and it's true. So now you can see that even God has (**haters**), and he will deal with them just as he did with the haters of old times, but notice that God is still here, **"and they aren't"**.

There's another old saying that goes: "**misery loves company**", and there's a lot of truth to it as well, which you will see in the biblical scripture below..........

Romans 1:32 (KJV)

32 Who knowing the judgment of God, that they which commit such things are worthy of death, not only do the same, but have pleasure in them that do them.

Notice that it says: not only do they do it themselves, but that they enjoy seeing others do it also, this is where "**misery loves company**", because people who are miserable usually like to see others miserable as well, and will encourage and entice others to commit acts of misery. It's the same exact principle that's used in (**Peer Pressure**), but with the opposite objective.

For example:

"**peer pressure**" is something that most people will use to get others to join them in doing something that they themselves aren't as comfortable in doing alone, usually with the intentions of having a good time. But in the "**misery loves company**" scenario, a person will encourage or entice others to commit acts of misery in hopes that they too will become as miserable as they themselves are, but in both cases, the individuals tend to identify with those like themselves.

This is a perfect example of why the leaders of society are so lenient to criminals, and are so willing to accept the unrighteousness of others, and will legislate atonement for the wicked, while provide excuses for the unrighteous, because they themselves are one in the same.

And the bible teaches us: **"how then can they judge righteously"**, because to condemn someone like this, would be the same as condemning themselves..........

Romans 2: (KJV)

1 Therefore thou art inexcusable, O man, whosoever thou art that judgest: for wherein thou judgest another, thou condemnest thyself; for thou that judgest doest the same things. 2 But we are sure that the judgment of God is according to truth against them which commit such things. 3 And thinkest thou this, O man, that judgest them which do such things, and doest the same, that thou shalt escape the judgment of God?

So you can be very certain, that God's judgment isn't in any ways like men, there are no escape clauses, so no one escapes! In fact, the only way to receive mercy and forgiveness, is to (**repent**), which means to reject your present life of unrighteousness, and start a new one that's righteous, but keep in mind that even though God forgives and shows mercy, you will still have to answer for what you've done, which means there will be punishment, "**to be determined by God**". Many people like to think that just because they repent they don't have to answer for what they've already done, but this isn't true. Repenting only means that you're remorseful for what you've done, and are willing to accept responsibility and change. There are many examples of this given throughout the Bible, but the most notable is the one of: (**David and Bathsheba**).

In this example, God forgives a man for killing another man so that he can have the man's wife, but the punishment that follows is very severe indeed, and costs him everything, even his own family and the child which they conceived..........

II Samuel 12: (KJV)

9 Wherefore hast thou despised the commandment of the LORD, to do evil in his sight? thou hast killed Uriah the Hittite with the sword, and hast taken his wife to be thy wife, and hast slain him with the sword of the children of Ammon. 10 Now therefore the sword shall never depart from thine house;

because thou hast despised me, and hast taken the
wife of Uriah the Hittite to be thy wife. 13 And
David said unto Nathan, I have sinned against the
LORD. And Nathan said unto David, The LORD also
hath put away thy sin; thou shalt not die.
14 Howbeit, because by this deed thou hast given
great occasion to the enemies of the LORD to
blaspheme, the child also that is born unto thee
shall surely die.

Another excellent example of punishment following
forgiveness is (**The Children of Israel**), who were
continually disobedient to God, and God often
forgave them, but would punish them with all sorts
of plagues, and sometimes even death.

So you can see that (**God forgives, but
punishment follows!**)
So in (**II Samuel 12**) Nathan explained to David,
that God forgave him, which was the only reason
that he was allowed to live, but as punishment," *the
sword would never leave his house*", which means
that there would always be death and destruction in
his household, "now keep this in mind" because it
goes back to what we learned earlier about the sins
of the parents, which can sometimes fall back on
their children, and it has nothing to do with God
punishing the children for what the parents did, but

it's due to association, just by the mere fact that the children are under the parents care, and so whatever the parents choose, will also be bestowed on the children, until the children are old enough to step out from under the parents care and choose for themselves.

This has caused so many people to have misplaced blame towards God for what happens to the children, they misunderstand God's roll in our lives. They don't understand that God can only come into our lives if we ask him to, but if you choose Satan, then he's allowed to come into your life as well, and the lives of your children, **"which would be at your request!"**

People automatically assume that just because God exists, he's in our lives, but it doesn't work that way, you must choose him.

Remember, there are two forces working in this world: **<u>Good</u>** and **<u>Evil</u>** (**God and Satan**) and if you are here, then you belong to one or the other, but there's no in-between, so you do have to choose, and those who do not choose, belong to Satan by default!

And regardless of what anyone tells you, **"you are responsible for your own actions"**.

Remember (**The Garden of Eden**), and how "**Eve**" was quick to point out that Satan tricked her, but in the end, who got punished..... (**Eve**). And remember "**Adam**" who was quick to point the finger at "Eve" when he was confronted, but likewise in the end, who got punished..... (**Adam**), while Satan sat back and laughed the whole time because he know his fate, but he wants to take as many people with him as possible.

Remember what we learned earlier? (**Misery loves company**), well Satan is the perfect example of that. So you can blame whoever you want, but the reality is "you are responsible for your actions", which means "**you are responsible for fixing you**", so as soon as you begin notice abnormalities in your **thoughts**, **actions**, or **behavior**, you should be prompt in addressing them, because Satan will set up shop in your heart and mind faster than you can imagine, and guess who "**will be responsible?**" But some will say: "well that's not fare" but actually it is, because as we learned earlier, Satan "**cannot make you do anything!**" (**He is only allowed to suggest**).

So even though he can be very influential in his suggestions, and powerful in his presentations, he still isn't allowed to "**make anyone do anything**" {**GOD FORBIDS!**} and has granted us free will to choose, even if we don't always like the choices. This is why you will always be responsible for your actions, especially since God has made it possible for us to know right from wrong (**righteousness**), even in a time of so many open interpretations of his word.

But the open interpretations has also lead to the many denominations and biblical translations that exist today, which has caused much confusion and weakened the integrity of the Bible, leaving people to question the validity of it all.

"However" there was a time when God's word was precious because there were no open versions or interpretations, there was only one vision........

I Samuel 3: (KJV)

1 And the child Samuel ministered unto the LORD before Eli. And the word of the LORD was precious in those days; *there was* no open vision.

But as you can see today, there are so many open visions/versions, and interpretations that everyone's left confused.

This is why I "**strongly**" suggest the KJV (**King James Version**). It is the closest thing that we have to the original word of God. It was first published in 1611 A.D. originally called "**THE HOLY BIBLE**" then in 1814 A.D. it was renamed the "**KING JAMES VERSION**" or the "**AUTHORIZED VERSION**" it is the first English bible ever printed in the United States. And every single version of the bible that exists today was inspired of it, but sadly, has been altered. So if you're interested in learning God's word, (*which everyone should be*) you really need to get it unaltered. This will eliminate the deception and confusion that drives so many people away from seeking God.

And believe it or not, seeking God is very important because you must seek God **"to see him"**. But there are so many people who have never seen God, and probably never will, because they never truly seek him, in fact, this is the very reason that **Atheist** and **Agnostics** exist in the first place, and besides that, seeking God is a specific requirement of his, and not only does he require that we seek him, but that we do it **"with all of our heart and all of our soul"**. This is why so many people will end up **Atheists** and **Agnostics**, because they sift through the Bible trying to prove that God doesn't exit, instead of seeking him.

Look at it this way: how do you know if a person is trustworthy, if you've never seen them in a situation to be trusted? There will always have to be some level of trust extended before this can be determined, "however", this doesn't mean that you should begin to trust people in the most critical situations, or with your most critical information, but you definitely cannot extend trust expressing distrust.

And when it comes to God **"Trust"** is everything, even the bible itself teaches that you must have faith before you can even began to please God:

Hebrews 11: (KJV)

6 But without faith *it is* impossible to please *him*: for he that cometh to God must believe that he is, and *that* he is a rewarder of them that diligently seek him.

So knowing this, you can see that it would be totally counterproductive to seek God from a mindset of trying to prove that he doesn't exist, because you will never ***see him***! ***Nor will he allow himself to be seen***! And to see God, you must seek him exactly as the Bible says.........

"WITH ALL OF YOUR HEART AND ALL OF YOUR SOUL"

Now this doesn't mean that you will see God physically, but God has a way of showing himself to you that will be unique to you "***and strictly for you***", which is why once you've seen God no one can tell you that he doesn't exist, because God is dealing with you, "***not them***". He is establishing his relationship with you, and does not have to prove anything to anyone else, although others will see his existence in your life.

But if you're living contrary to the Bible, then it's no wonder that you don't believe in God because you are not in his existence, "***and he definitely isn't in yours***!" And don't ever forget:

"IT IS US THAT NEED GOD, AND NOT THE OTHER WAY AROUND"

So don't make the same mistake that many others do, in thinking that God needs you.
And cursed are they that do as the infidels have done, by mocking the laws of God and creating new ones,
Such as legalizing marriage between (**Gays and Lesbians**), and exalting themselves as if they created man,
It just goes to show the evils men do, when Satan is the god that they answer to,
But men throughout history have established one fact:

(THE MORE WICKED THE DREAM, THE MORE WICKED THE ACT)

And these types of men lust for greed, glory power, which is typical in the dreams of weak men and cowards.
It's a sin that's plagued men since the very beginning of time, and it only gets worse with every generation left behind.
So the bible teaches us against glorying to be great, and desiring to be God is something that he hates.
Even Jesus did not except being glorified, and was prompt in correcting those who would even try,

He taught a leader must be gracious, courageous
and meek, and should lead by example the words
that he speak,
So this is the message that he would teach, as even
he once washed his fellowman's feet,
And the only one who should receive glory is God,
because to give life eternal is his not ours:

Mark 10: (KJV)

17And when he was gone forth into the way, there
came one running, and kneeled to him, and asked
him, Good Master, what shall I do that I may
inherit eternal life? **18** And Jesus said unto him,
Why callest thou me good? *there is* none good but
one, *that is*, God.

John 13: (KJV)

13 Ye call me Master and Lord: and ye say well; for
so I am. **14** If I then, *your* Lord and Master, have
washed your feet; ye also ought to wash one
another's feet. **15** For I have given you an example,
that ye should do as I have done to you.

So "clearly" Jesus was aware that he **"reign
supreme"**, as he stated in (**John 13:13**) **"Ye call me
Master and Lord: and ye say well; for *so* I am"**,
but then notice that he doesn't boast or brag, nor
does he seek praise and glory, and therefore has

established what's expected of us, especially if we are to obtain the status of a righteous leader, and anything else is unacceptable.

So "**no one**" should be calling themselves "**GOOD,GREAT**, or **HONERABLE**", or titles that glorify, nor should we refer to others as such in regards to righteousness, those who do are the fake ones, because Jesus said "**do as I have done**", so they are therefore not of God!

So what then (*if anything*) are all of the "*so-called*" Christians doing in the mist of all of the mayhem that society has conjured up? The answer is......

(*Absolutely nothing*), because true Christians are few, which means that very few people will do anything since very few people are true Christians, which is why you will see so many people in support of their **family members** and **friends** who are (**Gays and lesbians**), and because of this, very few people will be received by God:

Matthew (KJV)

7:21 Not every one that saith unto me, Lord, Lord, shall enter into the kingdom of heaven; but he that doeth the will of my Father which is in heaven. **22:14** For many are called, but few *are* chosen.

This means that everyone who has ever lived is called to righteousness, "but sadly" only a few will answer, and therefore, few will be chosen.

94

**"What about you?"... ..."Have you answered?".....
"Will you answer?"**

However, righteous men and women know that the
(Gay and Lesbian) lifestyle along with everything
else that's unrighteous in this world was foretold of
things to come, and therefore are aware that "**these
things must happen**" in order for God's system to
be fulfilled, as stated by Jesus............

Matthew 24: (KJV)

5 For many shall come in my name, saying, I am
Christ; and shall deceive many. 6 And ye shall hear
of wars and rumours of wars: see that ye be not
troubled: for all *these things* must come to pass, but
the end is not yet. 7 For nation shall rise against
nation, and kingdom against kingdom: and there
shall be famines, and pestilences, and earthquakes,
in divers places. 8 All these *are* the beginning of
sorrows.

So Jesus states that "*all these things* **must come to
pass**" and many of them are taking place even as
this book is being written. The only thing that we
really haven't seen yet, are many people claiming to
be Christ, but even then, that won't be the end,
because God's word has to be preached thoroughly

throughout the entire world, **"and then the end will come"**...........

Matthew 24:14 (KJV)
And this gospel of the kingdom shall be preached in all the world for a witness unto all nations; and then shall the end come.

"AND GOD'S PROPHECY WILL BE FULFILLED"

True Christians should not be discouraged as these things begin happen, but should instead continue in righteousness, and allow God's system to work.

..........A word from Jesus to the righteous..........

Matthew 24:6 (KJV)

"SEE THAT YE BE NOT TROUBLED"

NOTES

CHAPTER THREE

HOMOSEXUALITY

This chapter deals with the myths and deceptions surrounding Homosexuality, and exposes the truth which has been suppressed, hidden, or ignored. It explores the causes and effects of homosexuality through an in-depth look at Mankind, Nature, and Spirituality, which will shine a new light on the topic, revealing the truth surrounding Homosexuality.

Jesus states that there will be false prophets coming in his name, and will deceive many.

"Now imagine that" many of you are already deceived just by the foolishness of this society, so how much more so will you be, when those claiming to be Christ began to speak on matters of which you have no knowledge. For example: everyone knows where babies come from, and we all can determine boy from girl and male from female, so we do know that the natural process to procreate and continue life's cycle is through male and female, "but somehow" society has managed to deceive many into believing that the (**Gay and Lesbian**) lifestyle is acceptable, even after nature itself has emphatically established that the natural order of things is between male and female, whether it be in animals or humans.

"And quite honestly" I don't know that anything more can be said to enlighten those whom have chosen to accept the Gay and Lesbian lifestyle, since they seem to have very little understanding of the male and female's purpose in life. Otherwise, there are only a few reasons which immediately suggest themselves as to why someone would accept such behavior, which I hope isn't true. And the "*first*" being that they have chosen immorality regardless of the consequences, and are willing to accept the outcome of their fate by God. "*Secondly*", is that they do not believe that God is

CHAPTER THREE HOMOSEXUALITY   GAY AND LESBIAN THE TRUTH!

real, and can therefore do whatever they want with no real regard or consequences for their actions. And *thirdly*," which I hope "**is**" the reason for their behavior, is that they are just plain ignorant of God's laws, and have no knowledge of God what so ever.

"**Ignorance**" is the only excuse that God will accept as to why a person hasn't repented, because God is very clear that he will not destroy those whom are ignorant of morality and are unable to discern between righteousness and unrighteousness, which is why this book will be a death sentence to many of you, because by reading this book you now have the knowledge of righteousness and morality, and also where to find it," and therefore" can no longer claim ignorance as an excuse.

There's an example of this fact in one of the biblical stories of the Bible which is often referred to as (**Jonah and the Whale**). It's an awesome story that you should check out because it establishes this fact, and I'm sure you will enjoy it. But at the end of the story it makes this very point.............

Jonah 3: (KJV)

1 And the word of the LORD came unto Jonah the second time, saying, **2** Arise, go unto Nineveh, that great city, and preach unto it the preaching that I bid thee. **4** And Jonah began to enter into the city a day's journey, and he cried, and said, Yet forty

100

days, and Nineveh shall be overthrown. **5** So the people of Nineveh believed God, and proclaimed a fast, and put on sackcloth, from the greatest of them even to the least of them **6** For word came unto the king of Nineveh, and he arose from his throne, and he laid his robe from him, and covered *him* with sackcloth, and sat in ashes. **7** And he caused *it* to be proclaimed and published through Nineveh by the decree of the king and his nobles, saying, Let neither man nor beast, herd nor flock, taste any thing: let them not feed, nor drink water: **8** But let man and beast be covered with sackcloth, and cry mightily unto God: yea, let them turn every one from his evil way, and from the violence that *is* in their hands.

9 Who can tell *if* God will turn and repent, and turn away from his fierce anger, that we perish not? **10** And God saw their works, that they turned from their evil way; and God repented of the evil, that he had said that he would do unto them; and he did *it* not

Jonah 4: (KJV)

1 But it displeased Jonah exceedingly, and he was very angry. **4** Then said the LORD, Doest thou well to be angry? **11** And should not I spare Nineveh, that great city, wherein are more than sixscore thousand persons that cannot discern between their right hand and their left hand; and *also* much cattle?

So as you can see, God is always willing to accept repentance. He isn't out to get anyone, and does not take pleasure in punishing those whom have chosen sin. "In fact" if it were at all possible, he would rather that everyone would repent, especially those that have been devout sinners. "As Jesus explains" God gets more joy out of just one person who repents from a life of sin, than he does out of multiple numbers of people who have lived righteously and does not need repentance........

Luke 15: (KJV)

7 I say unto you, that likewise joy shall be in heaven over one sinner that repenteth, more than over ninety and nine just persons, which need no repentance.

"So once again" we see that God has made all sorts of provisions for anyone who wants to repent, and there isn't any excuse that you can give that's too much for God. Everyone is eligible," no matter what you've done", so don't let anyone tell you that you aren't worthy of repentance, "this is God's business" (HE) and he alone is judge and jury on this one! So to continue on in the ways of unrighteousness would be a blatant acceptance of immorality and an emphatic rejection of God, which is why you cannot take it personal or become offended when those seeking God have taken steps to remove you from their lives. It isn't that they don't love you, nor are they in any way claiming to be better than you, because everyone has issues in their lives that need to be resolved, but the bible teaches us that when a person chooses Christ, he or she must watch their associations, which is something that shouldn't be directed just towards the gay and lesbian community, but all forms of unrighteousness.

Ephesians 5: (KJV)

6 Let no man deceive you with vain words: for because of these things cometh the wrath of God upon the children of disobedience. 7 Be not ye therefore partakers with them. 8 For ye were sometimes darkness, but now *are ye* light in the Lord: walk as children of light:
9 (For the fruit of the Spirit *is* in all goodness and righteousness and truth;) 10 Proving what is acceptable unto the Lord. 11 And have no fellowship with the unfruitful works of darkness, but rather reprove *them*.

So not only should you be watching your associations, but you should also be telling others (when the opportunity permits) about their behavior! And as we reprove one another there shouldn't be any strife. If someone has to reprove you of your behavior with shouting or harsh and vulgar language, then this person has no part in the body of Christ, because Jesus "in no way" condones this kind of behavior, and in fact, anyone who does so, is operating on their own agenda, which has nothing to do with Christ.

True members of the body of Christ (Christians) are compassionate individuals, and would never speak in a demeaning or derogatory manner to others when conveying the gospel of Christ. They understand that this is God's business and not theirs, and therefore have no need to get worked up about someone rejecting Christ. So whenever preachers and priests, or any others claiming to be teachers of the gospel are harsh and loud, or demeaning in their delivery, "they are not of Christ" and have no business speaking on behalf of God since they themselves lack understanding of the very bible in which they claim to teach:

1Timothy 1: (KJV)

5 Now the end of the commandment is charity out of a pure heart, and *of* a good conscience, and *of* faith unfeigned: 6 From which some having

104

swerved have turned aside unto vain jangling; 7
Desiring to be teachers of the law; understanding
neither what they say, nor whereof they affirm. 8
But we know that the law *is* good, if a man use it
lawfully;
9 Knowing this, that the law is not made for a
righteous man, but for the lawless and disobedient,
for the ungodly and for sinners, for unholy and
profane, for murderers of fathers and murderers of
mothers, for manslayers, 10 For whoremongers,
for them that defile themselves with mankind, for
menstealers, for liars, for perjured persons, and if
there be any other thing that is contrary to sound
doctrine;

"In fact" if anyone desires to teach the word of God,
then the affirmation should always be the bible,
"and not their own opinion, views or doctrine"
which is why I will give you biblical facts to
support the revelations of this book, and it is also
why I cannot stress enough that you should only
reference the **"KING JAMES VERSION" or
(KJV)**, because everything else has been altered in
one way or another. Just remember what we learned
earlier about the alteration of words, and how it can
change the meaning of a message dramatically.
And also, as it relates to biblical matters (morality),
you should never be a respecter of persons, nor

should you revere titles, and in no way are we to be in awe of one another in Christianity, because we are all equal as brothers and sisters in the body of Christ, and are held accountable under the same law.

However, many Gays and Lesbians like to try and make the argument that there aren't many laws in the bible that speaks against their behavior, which is a very weak argument for two reasons, and the first being that, if there is just one law that says it's wrong, then that's enough, and you don't need another law to say so. And the second reason is that, there are many laws all throughout the Bible which not only condemns the behavior of Gays and lesbians, but also condemns other types of inappropriate behaviors, all at the same time.

For example, look at the verse above, **(1Timothy 1: 9) "Knowing this, that the law is not made for a righteous man, but for the lawless and disobedient, for the ungodly and for sinners, for unholy and profane, for murderers of fathers and murderers of mothers, for manslayers, 10 For whoremongers, for them that defile themselves with mankind, for menstealers, for liars, for perjured persons, and if there be any other thing that is contrary to sound doctrine;".**

So when it says: (**for them that defile themselves with mankind**), this speaks directly to the Gay and Lesbian community, and if that weren't enough, then the very end of this verse also speaks to the condemnation of Homosexuality, and anything else that is unrighteous and immoral, as it states: (**and if there be any other thing that is contrary to sound doctrine**).

And you do know that the Bible is the soundest doctrine that there is.... *right*?

So these two verses are just an example of the many verses in the Bible that condemns Homosexuality, but these two verses not only condemn Homosexuality, but multiple sins as well. For example, the verse above that states: (**for them that defile themselves with mankind**), also includes (*MMA fighters, Boxers, Strippers*) and many others, even heterosexuals who participate in inappropriate sexual behavior, because all of these are acts where individuals defile themselves involving another person as the verse above describes. And to defile oneself with mankind simply means to: (*abuse, mar, scar, impair, violate, degrade, pervert, and degenerate*) or to use oneself for an unnatural or unintended purpose in which mankind was not created, and mankind was not created to do any of the above mentioned defamations.

But everyone sins in some way or another every single day, regardless of how *"just or good"* they may think they are, and therefore falls short of God's grace and are held accountable under the same law which God handed down to Moses for an everlasting, (generation to generation):

Ecclesiastes 7: (KJV)

20 For *there is* not a just man upon earth, that doeth good, and sinneth not.

Exodus 12: (KJV)

49 One law shall be to him that is homeborn, and unto the stranger that sojourneth among you. **50** Thus did all the children of Israel; as the LORD commanded Moses and Aaron, so did they.

But in today's world there are many denominations with many different views and many different values, and they all operate on very different principles, which is why you should always be very careful about giving your endorsement as a member of any church or organization as it relates to Christianity, which actually belongs to God, because whatever that church or organization stands for, then so will you. And you definitely do not

want to represent something that God is against. And even though it's ok to go to these establishments seeking God, or to attend their services, you will still need to watch your endorsement. You must keep in mind that many of these organization aren't even about God or Christianity anymore, but instead are organizations where the leaders have made it about themselves, and have become (their own religion), and if you're serving them, then you aren't serving God!
"In fact" most of these religious organizations and denominations aren't even recognized by Jesus, whom has to give his approval before God will even begin to accept them. So even though they may do all these things that they claim are in Jesus name, they still aren't recognized by him, and therefore do not have his approval................

Matthew 7: (KJV)

22 Many will say to me in that day, Lord, Lord, have we not prophesied in thy name? and in thy name have cast out devils? and in thy name done many wonderful works? 23 And then will I profess unto them, I never knew you: depart from me, ye that work iniquity.

"Imagine that" Mostly all of these churches and organizations that think that they're doing good, aren't even aware that they're not recognized by

Jesus, but if they were actually reading the Bible instead of quoting it, then they would.

One of the biggest reasons that these churches and organization and people in general aren't recognized by Jesus, is because they think that they can serve God any way they want, "which is totally ridicules", God has guidelines and rules.

You couldn't even represent the company that you work for any way that you want; even they have guidelines and rules. For example, Your place of employment would never allow you to come to work wearing the competitor's attire, nor would they allow you to use certain language, or set your own policies and hours, this would be totally unacceptable and highly insubordinate, and we all know what happens when an employee is insubordinate...... don't we?

It's even much more so with God!

He has policies and procedures in place that we must adhere to. You cannot do whatever you want, nor act however you want, but instead you must change. You must redefine yourself into that which is acceptable to God, which is what is known as (**Being Born Again**). To be born again, means that you must change your way of thinking and conduct from that which society has established, to that which God has established.

Many people will even attempt to teach the Gospel by world standards instead of God's, and somehow

110

they really seem to think that this is acceptable, but you cannot sink to the world's level of conduct, claiming it to be your way of reaching the people, or a particular group of people, "this is unacceptable", and it's not what Jesus taught or displayed. And in fact, it's actually contradictory to the gospel of Christ, because to do this means to act in a way that the gospel teaches against, and God doesn't lower his standards for anyone, but instead requires that we raise ours.

So if anyone has a problem with receiving the gospel of Christ from those whom conduct themselves in the manor that God has required, then they can either accept or reject it, but lowering God's standards," **definitely isn't an option"**, and will only result in your removal from God's grace. "But strangely enough" not only do most people reject God because they can't live in sin and receive god at the same time, but they will also insist that they must see some sort of great sign or miracle before they will accept or believe that God is real. But God won't be persuaded by any of us to work wonders or miracle so that we may believe what's written in the bible, because first of all none of us are that important, and second, if you don't believe the Bible, then won't believe God. Much like the story of (**Lazarus**), where a man died and went to "Hell" and was in such torment that he cried out to the heavens asking that someone would be sent to

111

his remaining family members to warn them of
"Hell", in hopes that they would repent and avoid
ending up there to suffer with him:

Luke 16: (KJV)

19 There was a certain rich man, which was clothed
in purple and fine linen, and fared sumptuously
every day: **20** And there was a certain beggar
named Lazarus, which was laid at his gate, full of
sores, **21** And desiring to be fed with the crumbs
which fell from the rich man's table: moreover the
dogs came and licked his sores. **22** And it came to
pass, that the beggar died, and was carried by the
angels into Abraham's bosom: the rich man also
died, and was buried; **23** And in hell he lift up his
eyes, being in torments, and seeth Abraham afar
off, and Lazarus in his bosom. **24** And he cried and
said, Father Abraham, have mercy on me, and send
Lazarus, that he may dip the tip of his finger in
water, and cool my tongue; for I am tormented in
this flame. **25** But Abraham said, Son, remember
that thou in thy lifetime receivedst thy good things,
and likewise Lazarus evil things: but now he is
comforted, and thou art tormented. **26** And beside
all this, between us and you there is a great gulf
fixed: so that they which would pass from hence to
you cannot; neither can they pass to us, that *would*

come from thence. **27** Then he said, I pray thee therefore, father, that thou wouldest send him to my father's house: **28** For I have five brethren; that he may testify unto them, lest they also come into this place of torment. **29** Abraham saith unto him, They have Moses and the prophets; let them hear them. **30** And he said, Nay, father Abraham: but if one went unto them from the dead, they will repent. **31** And he said unto him, If they hear not Moses and the prophets, neither will they be persuaded, though one rose from the dead.

So as you can see, people have not changed since Biblical times, because everyone wants to see some great sign or miracle before they are willing to believe, but just as those of Biblical times had **(Moses and the Prophets)** and did not believe, you have **(The Holy bible)** "the equivalent" and will not believe.
"Furthermore" having prophets and seeing miracles really isn't necessary because everyone "including gays and lesbians" know when they're doing wrong, because God has given all of mankind an intuitive knowledge of right and wrong, which we inherited from God's chosen of Biblical times, to be handed down from generation to generation, for perpetual generations, so that when we hear the truth "*we know it*".....................

113

Hebrews 8: (KJV)

10 For this *is* the covenant that I will make with the house of Israel after those days, saith the Lord; I will put my laws into their mind, and write them in their hearts: and I will be to them a God, and they shall be to me a people:

Titus 2: (KJV)

11 For the grace of God that bringeth salvation hath appeared to all men, **12** Teaching us that, denying ungodliness and worldly lusts, we should live soberly, righteously, and godly, in this present world;

So we have all been warned, and the day is coming when repentance will be too late, and no one knows when that day is. Even Jesus himself says: "*he doesn't know*", and if he doesn't know "*then neither will we*"

Matthew 24: (KJV)

27 For as the lightning cometh out of the east, and shineth even unto the west; so shall also the coming of the Son of man be. **30** And then shall appear the sign of the Son of man in heaven: and then shall all the tribes of the earth mourn, and they shall see the Son of man coming in the clouds of heaven with power and great glory. **31** And he shall send his angels with a great sound of a trumpet, and they shall gather together his elect from the four winds, from one end of heaven to the other. **36** But of that day and hour knoweth no *man*, no, not the angels of heaven, but my Father only. **38** For as in the days that were before the flood they were eating and drinking, marrying and giving in marriage, until the day that Noe entered into the ark, **39** And knew not until the flood came, and took them all away; so shall also the coming of the Son of man be. **42** Watch therefore: for ye know not what hour your Lord doth come.

So don't let anyone tell you that they know, or that they've figured it out. In fact "anyone that makes this claim should be counted as a fool" because if Jesus himself says that he and the angels of heaven don't know, then it's absolutely impossible for us lowly undeserving insignificant human beings to know. And he goes even further to say that only his Father (God) knows, as reiterated below............

Mark 13: (KJV)

32 But of that day and *that* hour knoweth no man, no, not the angels which are in heaven, neither the Son, but the Father. **33** Take ye heed, watch and pray: for ye know not when the time is.

I guess those whom say they know, somehow think that they are God?

But you can know one thing for certain, which is.... when you see Jesus in the flesh, "**repentance**" will be too late!

Understand that, "**life is a gift**", and with it are so many possibilities and wonders that can be achieved, which is evident in all that exists today, but as with any gift, there are rules and responsibilities that go with it, and we should be respectable, responsible and appreciative enough to be worthy of it. Can you imagine giving your child a gift and watching as they abuse, misuse and destroy it with no regards for the love and thoughtfulness in which the gift was given. What would you do if you gave your child a toy and that child proceeded to strike another sibling over the head repeatedly with it? I'm pretty sure that any responsible normal thinking parent would remove that toy from the child and discipline would follow.....right?

So what then, do you think God is going to do in that same scenario, especially with him being our "**Father**" which is in heaven?

And every society, as leaders of the people, has that same roll of responsibility over the people that a parent has over a child, which makes it even sadder

116

when you consider the fact that the leaders of society have failed the people in this roll. A roll in which they have proven to be very lousy parents. Let's take a look at God's structure for mankind in the very beginning.

So in the beginning, the man and woman were given specific assignments as equals by God, and as a couple they would become as one, to share in the responsibilities of those assignment.

The man was given the assignment of establishing the world that God had created, such as tilling the ground, naming the animals, and even designing and maintaining the Garden of Eden. And the woman "no less" was to assist the man in these assignments, as well as rearing children, which is why she was created as the feminine gender, to conceive and bear children. She was also given the feminine structure and demeanor necessary in rearing and nurturing children, as it is quite obvious that men were not designed to do. So let's take a look at the Biblical account below...........

Genesis 2: (KJV)

7 And the LORD God formed man *of* the dust of the ground, and breathed into his nostrils the breath of life; and man became a living soul. 8 And the LORD God planted a garden eastward in Eden; and there he put the man whom he had formed. 15 And the LORD God took the man, and put him

into the garden of Eden to dress it and to keep it.
18 And the LORD God said, *It is* not good that the
man should be alone; I will make him an help meet
for him. **20** And Adam gave names to all cattle, and
to the fowl of the air, and to every beast of the field;
but for Adam there was not found an help meet for
him. **21** And the LORD God caused a deep sleep to
fall upon Adam, and he slept: and he took one of
his ribs, and closed up the flesh instead thereof; **22**
And the rib, which the LORD God had taken from
man, made he a woman, and brought her unto the
man.

23 And Adam said, This *is* now bone of my bones,
and flesh of my flesh: she shall be called Woman,
because she was taken out of Man. **24** Therefore
shall a man leave his father and his mother, and
shall cleave unto his wife: and they shall be one
flesh.

Genesis 1: (KJV)

27 So God created man in his *own* image, in the
image of God created he him; male and female
created he them. **28** And God blessed them, and
God said unto them, Be fruitful, and multiply, and
replenish the earth, and subdue it: and have
dominion over the fish of the sea, and over the fowl

of the air, and over every living thing that moveth upon the earth.

So as you can see, God said to them "**Be fruitful, and multiply**" (meaning to be intimate and have children) and to "**replenish the earth, and subdue it:**" and to have dominion over every living thing on earth. So they were to take control of the earth to manage and maintain it, and to keep things working together. They would subdue this earth together, neither being the authority over the other, but would do it under God's guidance together. It wasn't until the woman's fall from grace that God allowed men to rule over women. "As a matter of fact "when the woman proved to be disloyal and disobedient, God punished her in a way that would affect every woman from that moment in time until this present day, as shown below...............

Genesis 2: (KJV)

13 And the LORD God said unto the woman, What *is* this *that* thou hast done? And the woman said, The serpent beguiled me, and I did eat. **16** Unto the woman he said, I will greatly multiply thy sorrow and thy conception; in sorrow thou shalt bring forth children; and thy desire *shall be* to thy husband, and he shall rule over thee.

So this punishment to the woman was "**severe**", and would affect all woman from that day forward, which is why women suffer greatly during pregnancy, from conception to birth, such as: (**labor pains, morning sickness, delivery, etc**), and it is also why men have been given dominance over women, as God stated: (**thy desire *shall be* to thy husband, and he shall rule over thee**). It is an "inherited sin" of women handed down by God as a consequence for disobedience, which affects all women by way of heritage, due to the fact that every woman shares the same genetics as (**Eve**) the first woman, just as every man share the same genetics as (**Adam**) the first man.

So just as our parents have passed their genes down to us, we also pass our genes down to our children....and so on, all the way back to Adam and Eve.

Ever notice how much some children will closely resemble their parents? Some will even resemble their parents so much so, that we call them a (spitting image), which means that the two are almost identical.

We even pass down our characteristic traits, which will cause a child to display some similar characteristics as that of their parents, which has lead to such expressions as (*like father like son*) and (*like mother like daughter*).

120

These expressions are indicative of our ability to pass down our genetics from one generation to the next, and it's all hereditary.

And this is how it works: during conception, our genes (DNA) are passed down through the bloodline, as well as some of our characteristic traits (spirituality), which is sometimes more noticeable in some than others.

It is during conception that the male or female gender will be determined, and it is also during this period that the genetics will be established. The genetics can pass down characteristic traits consisting of mental and physical attributes, such as (demeanor, skin tone, eye tent, hair color, vocal inflections, height, and so on) but it does not pass down personal preferences, nor does it mix or match genders. For example:

- If the sperm carrying an **X** chromosome fertilizes the egg, a **girl** will be conceived.
- If the sperm carrying a **Y** chromosome fertilizes the egg, then a **boy** will be conceived.

But it does not fertilize the egg with (50% **X** and 50%**Y**) or any other combination of gender mixing. Another more blunt way of putting it is:

- If you are born with a vagina, ovaries and a uterus, you're a **female**.
- If you are born with a penis, prostate and testicles, then you're a **male**.

So to be gay or lesbian isn't some genetically induced state before birth, but instead, it is a choice made long after puberty, and any decisions made before that, are strictly experimental.

Here's a rule of thumb to go by whenever you find it difficult to distinguish between that which you control, and that of which you have no control: (**Any situation that requires your approval for participation, is within your control**), and you are not bound against your will. But any situation which occurs regardless of your approval, (**is one of which you have no control**), such as genetics, or sickness and disease, whereas you have no control. So " In other words" you could not have chosen the color your hair, height, skin tone, or your eye tint, and "God forbid" should you ever become stricken with cancer, aids, or any other life threatening diseases, you will not be able to say "**I choose not to have this disease**" and have it go away.

These are all conditions in which you have no control, much to the contrary of being Gay or Lesbian, whereas a simple yes or no is all that it requires.

The leaders of our societies (which are predominantly men) are primarily the blame for all of the confusion surrounding the gay and lesbian lifestyle.
Even as God has allowed men to rule, they are quick to relinquish those roles to women, as they themselves become more feminized, which actually leaves women no other choice but to step into these roles of leadership.

"It would be better that a child took the wheel, than to let a despondent man crash"

Much praise should be given to women, whom have stepped into the leadership roles of men to maintain the family and business of society, which has been relinquished to them by men, or "taken by default". But even though men have done poorly, it cannot be left entirely up to women; "after all" it was the demeanor of a woman that started the whole down spiral of humanity in the first place. But it does show that women have a very valuable input that cannot be denied, and definitely should not be overlooked. "The fact of the matter is" it takes both sexes to get the correct balance in subduing, maintaining and replenishing the earth, which is why God said *"It is not good that man should be alone; I will make him an help meet for him."*

And we all know that two men (Gays) could never replenish the earth, nor could two women (Lesbians). So when God chose to create a "help meet" (**companion, spouse, PARTNER**) for man, he chose a gender that was totally opposite of man, but yet would be completely complimentary to him, in subduing, maintaining and replenishing the earth. This is known as (**the natural order of things**) and anything else is (**the unnatural order**).
"In other words" a male and female are designed for one another, mentally, physically, spiritually and emotionally, whereas being Gay or Lesbian is strictly a sexually oriented relationship.

Many will disagree, and disagree as they may, here's the reason why:

As it was briefly explained earlier "You" as a male or female can love someone of the same sex, or enjoy the same sex's company, and even prefer spending most of your time with the same sex. This is simply a choice of preference in socializing, and there's nothing Gay or Lesbian about it, but once you began to have intimate interests in the same sex, then it turns "**unnatural**", and puts you into the category of Gay or Lesbian, which is defined by sexual orientation. "So once again" If you remove the sexual orientation it's completely natural, "but reinsert it," and you're back to a Gay and Lesbian scenario. This is the perfect explanation of why being Gay or Lesbian is strictly of a sexual nature. It can only be Gay or Lesbian with the implementation of an intimate attraction in the same sex.

And as for men acting feminine, and women masculine, this is another whole different set of issues going on, which may not necessarily be associated with one's sexual preference, but could be attributed to a wide variety of reasons, "which are way too many to name", but the one thing we do know is that many Gays and Lesbians mimic the opposite sex out of envy, which is to say that the Gay men envy women and the Lesbians envy men, and not so much out of hatefulness, but infectious instead. I guess the best way to describe it is like this: remember when you were a kid and had a favorite character that you liked to watch (your hero), and you would mimic them routinely, even on Halloween you wanted to dress like them, and at Christmas you expected gifts of toys, clothes, and games of them.... or maybe you've never gone through that faze, but what about as a teen, because if you were like most teens then there had to be someone that you liked? Maybe some singer, actor, or dancer that you were in total awe of, even to the point of wanting to look like them, dress, sing, dance or even act like them.

So basically that's what's going on when (**Cross dressers, Trans-genders, Gays and Lesbians**) mimicking the opposite sex.

But let's take a step back for a moment, to take a look at men, starting with the very first man ever to exist (**Adam**), whom was punished for being influence by a woman to be disobedient to God. He allowed a woman to influence him against what he knew to be right. So like many people today, he chose to follow a person rather than God, even though he was instructed "face to face" by God himself.

It just goes to show, that mankind's nature will always be self-serving, which is why it's extremely important that we humble ourselves before God. But many people will use the excuse that God may not exist, "as if it really matters" because we all know that if you can't accept his word (**The Bible**) then you won't accept him. So Just like Adam and Eve, you've already chosen to do whatever you like, which only further proves the wickedness of mankind, whose thoughts are (continuously evil), and so much so, that even God himself once regretted creating man:

Genesis 6: (KJV)

5 And GOD saw that the wickedness of man *was* great in the earth, and *that* every imagination of the thoughts of his heart *was* only evil continually. **6** And it repented the LORD that he had made man on the earth, and it grieved him at his heart. **7** And the LORD said, I will destroy man whom I have created from the face of the earth; both man, and beast, and the creeping thing, and the fowls of the air; for it repenteth me that I have made them.

Imagine that, being so wicked that God regrets he created you, which only proves that we as human beings will always refuse to do what is right, except that we humble ourselves before God. "Eve" is the perfect example of this, because she allowed Satan to convince her that she could be like God, if she would eat from the tree that she should not, so she jumped at the chance and disobeyed God, and never realized that she was being robbed, allowing Satan to destroy her and God's relationship, when she should have replied: **"WHY DON'T YOU DO IT!"** then she would have known that **"THE DEVIL IS A LIE"**, it would have given God the glory just like Jesus' reply.......

Luke 4: (KJV)

8 And Jesus answered and said unto him, Get thee behind me, Satan: for it is written, Thou shalt worship the Lord thy God, and him only shalt thou serve.

127

That would have been all that Eve needed to say, which would be a great response even today.
Just imagine the power of that phrase. You could use it in many situations where someone would try and get you to do something that goes against God. For example: if someone approached you to entice you with homosexuality, all you'd have to say is *"Get thee behind me, Satan: for it is written, Thou shalt worship the Lord thy God, and him only shalt thou serve "*.

"Just think" if Eve would have dealt with the serpent that way we wouldn't be in this situation.

And we know that the serpent which spoke to Eve was Satan, (for two reasons):

(1) Serpents can't talk

(2) Serpent is also another name for Satan, whom is on earth to deceive the whole world, just as he did with Eve.........

Revelation 12: (KJV)

9 And the great dragon was cast out, that old serpent, called the Devil, and Satan, which deceiveth the whole world: he was cast out into the earth, and his angels were cast out with him.

128

So as you can see, Satan has about as many names as he has faces, which is why you really have to watch people, because many people have that same dragon, serpent like mentality as Satan, which stands to reason considering most people serve Satan.

But even though Eve allowed herself to be deceived in her inappropriate desire to be like God, Adam should have never followed suit, this was Adam's chance to glorify God with loyalty respect and honor, but instead, he responded with the same characteristic of men today, by choosing to follow the created instead of the creator.

And Satan knew that Adam would be more of a challenge in a direct approach, being that he was created masculine, and therefore would offer more of a resistance. So he used subtlety in his approach by choosing Eve, whom was created the feminine of the two, and would prove to be more susceptible to an attack on her morals and allegiance, and would also be instrumental in seducing Adam into disobedience. And as history has proven, this worked very well, and continues to work even unto this day.

Satan is a master manipulator, so you must avoid all temptations, because it only takes an ounce of temptation to equal a ton of regret, and due to the fact that mankind is unable to correct and govern themselves, the proper (**Christian**) structure handed down by God to Jesus and Paul to be delivered to the world, are as follows:

- God is the head of Christ.
- Christ is the head of men.
- Men are the head of the women.
- And women are then the head of children.

1 Corinthians 1: (KJV)

1 Paul, called *to be* an apostle of Jesus Christ through the will of God, and Sosthenes *our* brother,

1 Corinthians 11: (KJV)

2 Now I praise you, brethren, that ye remember me in all things, and keep the ordinances, as I delivered *them* to you. **3** But I would have you know, that the head of every man is Christ; and the head of the woman *is* the man; and the head of Christ *is* God.

But in today's world, you can see that there's a total breakdown in our society of this structure, and it's largely due to the fact that everyone has chosen to follow man instead of God, which is why families are torn, broken, and dysfunctional. And the first offender of this sin are men, whom we have learned from the verse above are responsible as head of the woman/household.

So it is their responsibility to ensure the safety, support, and wellbeing of the family "**PERIOD!**" And whenever a child is born, there's a father out there somewhere who has a responsibility to that child, (**like it or not!**). So to just walk away as if he had no part in it (**is totally unacceptable!**). And not only is it wrong, but it's also a "sin" unto God! Now I know that there are men out there who probably can't relate, "So let me put it in perspective for you":

1) First there's God.
2) Then Jesus Christ.
3) The church, (not what see today, but the real church as described in the bible).
4) Your parents.
5) Local government.
6) And national government.

As you can see, your government is last in line among those of whom you should be seeking for counsel, and it's primarily due to the fact that the government is void of Godliness. The government is an establishment headed by Satan, which is why it is filled with antichrist governing (**governing against the principle of Christ**). Remember earlier we learned that Satan and his angels were cast down to earth to devour mankind? Well it appears as if most of them landed in government, and whenever there's a turnover in government, that same type of demonic spirited individual is rotated into those positions to perpetuate the destruction of God's system, and mankind.

But it isn't blatant, it's not like they all sit around in boardrooms plotting and planning on how to overthrow God's system and destroy the world, "**no not at all**", it's more subtle, it's done by the mere fact that they have chosen not to serve God, but rather themselves, and have refused to acknowledge God in everything that they do, which is the objective of (**Satan's**). And that's what makes them "**Antichrist**", servers of Satan, (**DEVILS**).

And even though these individuals are elected by the people, it is their deceptive manipulative behavior of the people that has led them to being elected, which is no wonder when you have a masterful deceiver such as Satan, and a nation of infidels that simply refuse to seek and accept God.

"A nation ignorant of righteousness, morality and common sense"

So to those of you who may not have known God's status in this world "now you know".

And even though it would appear as though the government was the highest authority in the land,

132

when it comes to righteousness and morality, their actually the lowest!
There is no authority or intelligence beyond God.................

Proverbs 21: (KJV)

30 *There is* no wisdom nor understanding nor counsel against the LORD.

Jeremiah 23: (KJV)

24 Can any hide himself in secret places that I shall not see him? saith the LORD. Do not I fill heaven and earth? saith the LORD.

Isaiah 45: (KJV)

22 Look unto me, and be ye saved, all the ends of the earth: for I *am* God, and *there is* none else.

Romans 14: (KJV)

11 For it is written, *As* I live, saith the Lord, every knee shall bow to me, and every tongue shall confess to God.

Revelation 22: (KJV)

13 I am Alpha and Omega, the beginning and the end, the first and the last.

And knowing this, men will still desire to be God, rather than to obey him, furthering the disrespect and blasphemy which is fueled by their contempt for God's authority. But this isn't the first generation of men to defile God's blessings. You will find all throughout history, time and time again that men have always been perverse in their existence, in every aspect of life, especially as it relates to the Gay and Lesbian community. In fact, there wouldn't even be a Gay and Lesbian community except that men have failed the family, of which they were designated to be the head.

Men and their perverted desires have oppressed, abused, confused and misused the family to the point of total destruction; they have committed these acts on their children, other's children, their wives', women, and even each other, **"with no remorse"**.

Many of you are probably wondering *"where does this behavior come from*?" And quite simple, it's just a matter of suggestion......"*that's right*"......

"Satan suggests and people accept".

The bible describes it as...... **(People giving heed to seducing spirits of the devil)**

I Timothy 4: (KJV)

1 Now the Spirit speaketh expressly, that in the latter times some shall depart from the faith, giving heed to seducing spirits, and doctrines of devils;

So because people have departed from the faith (**God**), this is very easy for Satan to do, because he can appear in many forms, but most often it's subliminal. He uses subtlety to divert the attention away from himself, because he needs you to believe that it is your thoughts and not his, because that will cause you to let your guard down and be more acceptable to the suggestions, which you must admit, "is really cleaver".

Look at it this way, if you wanted to get someone to do something that you didn't want pointing back to you, you wouldn't force them to do it, nor would you participate in the act, because even thought they would be ultimately responsible, you will always be considered an accomplice. But if you were to instigate or manipulate someone into doing something, then they will be considered as having acted alone, when in reality you were an accomplice in getting them to do it.

And that's exactly what Satan does. He does this by using individuals whom have received and accepted his suggestions. It's like a relay race, the person with the baton of unrighteousness, just passes it on the neat person, who then takes off to give it to the next, and so on.

Society is structured on this same principle, which it uses in every aspect of society, "especially marketing". This society will use subtlety with lies and deceit and call it (**Brilliant Marketing**), which is totally unacceptable to God, (**but accepted by Satan**), and of course many of you!

This is just one of the many evidences that Satan heads this system of society, which has shown to incorporate and legislate many of Satan's practices, "most recently" being the legalization of "**Gay and Lesbian marriages!**"

So all of society's leaders: (**President, Congress, House of Representatives, Governors of States, local City Councils** and **School Boards** along with many **Citizens**), have collectively decided that God is wrong, and that marriage isn't just between a man and a woman, and have rescinded God's laws against the Gay and Lesbian lifestyle......"WOW!"

Let's take a look at another example of Satan's practices in society: "Lawyers" (**Attorney**), these individuals also submit to Satan as well. A lawyer will work to free individuals whom are guilty, and cycle them back into society with the assistance of (**judges and courts**), which allows them to continue their demonic behavior on other innocent citizens. And even though the guilty are suppose to be held accountable, it's not a sin to defend a guilty individual whom acknowledges their crime and are willing to accept full responsibility of their actions and the punishment that follows, "**even God does this**", it's called (*forgiveness*), but an Attorney who defends guilty individuals as though they are

innocent, and lies, deceive, and mislead to
accomplish it, is a "**DEVIL**" by all accounts!
Now with that said, let's get back to the "**Gay and
Lesbian marriages**" which society has established
in legislation, this too by all accounts is an "**unholy
union**", and if it is unholy then it is unrighteous,
and if it is unrighteous then it is unrecognized by
God, if it is unrecognized by God then it is wrong,
(**unacceptable!**).
And I'm quite sure that many of you have had
numerous encounters with your conscience on this
matter, and will continue to do so if righteousness is
at all in you, but you will have to be patient and
remain open minded, and allow righteousness to
work within you.
But for those who lack righteousness, (**Devout
Sinners**), they have already chosen their fate by
serving Satan (**The Devil**), and by lying to
themselves and everyone around them to the point
of spreading hypocrisy, and destroying their own
conscience, so that nothing concerning
righteousness will ever disturb their conscience
again...............

I Timothy 4: (KJV)

1 Now the Spirit speaketh expressly, that in the
latter times some shall depart from the faith, giving
heed to seducing spirits, and doctrines of devils; **2**

Speaking lies in hypocrisy; having their conscience
seared with a hot iron;

So the verse above describes them as (**having their
conscience seared with a hot iron**).
And their objective was to make sure that their
conscience never restored order again, which is
what your conscience does.
Remember what we learned earlier, God said that
he would write his word in our hearts and in our
minds, well this actually started with the "**children
of Israel**", which was also known as the "**house of
Israel**"........

Hebrews 8: (KJV)

10 For this *is* the covenant that I will make with the
house of Israel after those days, saith the Lord; I
will put my laws into their mind, and write them in
their hearts: and I will be to them a God, and they
shall be to me a people:

But this was then extended to all of mankind as God
allowed for repentance and became the God of all
of mankind. So the the purpose of our conscience is
to disturb us when we are wrong, and remind us of
the truth, which is why you will feel guilty when
you've done something wrong, but it only works for
those who have not "*seared their conscience with a
hot iron*".

138

This is why those who still have a conscience can't understand how anyone could be:

(Pedophile, Rapist, Gay or Lesbian, Racist, corrupt, murderer, etc)

Because these are all things that disturb the conscience, so it leaves only **"two"** reasons that these individuals will exhibit this behavior:

1) *They have seared their conscience.*
2) *They have no knowledge of the truth, (God).*

But as for this system and society, you will never receive the truth, because the truth isn't in them, so how can they deliver it to you? However, if you desire to know the truth, then "righteousness" is in you; and being "Gay or Lesbian" will not keep God from you, but it does require that you seek him, and you don't even have to believe, "*just seek him with an open mind*", and he will do the rest.
So we don't have to be as Adam, and have our surroundings cursed, causing life to be hard and laborious, simply because we refuse to acknowledge God first.
"Remember", God cursed the ground due to Adam's disobedience in listening to Eve, and he caused Adam to have to work harder than necessary to get food and preserve his life.

139

Now what if God did that to us today?
What if God decided that because of our behavior
he's going to suspend the rain, the sun, or wind, or
even allow the entire earth to become barren, *do
you think you could handle that?*
This is something that needs to be considered while
taking God's blessings for granted.
And if you don't believe in God....."Remember","
man didn't create this world", but whoever did is
probably more than capable of "*shutting it
down!*".....or at least, can make it "**hell**" for us!
But then of course there are those who believe that
nature created us out of itself, which just happens to
be a very comical concept. Man created by nature is
the story Agnostics and Atheists tell, Scientists even
believe the elements of nature created animals as
well, but they also confess that some animals are
becoming extinct....but how can this be....nature
would just make more wouldn't you think?
So why have the elements of nature stopped
creating us out of itself?
Scientists seem to believe there's no longer a need
because the world is populated well.
Have you ever known anything to quit growing
because it's populated well, even fruit will not quit
growing because trees have populated themselves.
But Scientists insist that the elements of space were
all aligned perfectly in time, but this would be like
saying that the elements of nature are not

improperly aligned, but the Sun, Moon, and Rain
are all the same today as they were back then, in
fact the only thing that continues change is the story
of Scientists!
Here's an example of the logic they suggest: Let's
say that you have all of the ingredients to bake a
cake, so you mix it and put it in an oven, then set
the right temperature for the allotted amount of
time, and it still comes out just batter, **"no cake"**,
because even though all of the elements were right,
there's enough cake in the world, **"so it won't bake"**
(*silly, I know*).
The earth and space still have all of the elements
today that were there thousands of years ago when
it used to **"make humans"** (*according to scientist*)
so what's wrong? I guess we're just not baking long
enough! "Anyway" enough fun with that!
You should be more concerned with seeking God,
and allowing him to show himself to you, which
should be done just between you and God, do not
involve: (**preachers, pastors, priests, popes**) or
any other so called **"man of the cloth wanna-be"**,
because the last thing you need is more confusion!
You will need to take a minute and set some time
aside for yourself, to be alone and have a
conversation with God. Just let him know that you
want him to come into your life, this can be done
kneeling, sitting, standing, or even lying down,
"there's no required position", although kneeling or

bowing your head is a sign of humility, a physical showing of respect and humility for God's authority, and not for those around you but for God himself. But if you truly respect God's authority, "*he knows!*" And there's no time frame while doing this, it can be as short or as long as you need it to be, but it should definitely be your own words and from the "*heart*", with no background distractions. Most people will close their eyes to avoid distractions as well.

And God already knows everything about you and all that you've done, "*so you can't shock him*", so don't be afraid to speak on whatever you choose. And even if you're not sure that you're ready for change at this point in your life, it's still a very good thing to do, as long as you are sure that you do want God in your life, and the sooner the better because God has a knack for appearing at just the right time, and not necessarily when you call, which just happens to be one of the more frustrating conditions that you will experience while seeking God, "*and it does take some getting used to*", it's also the single most popular reason given as to why people will stray from seeking God.

So when you pray, use the example and guidelines that are set forth by Jesus, and not men:

Matthew 6: (KJV)

5 And when thou prayest, thou shalt not be as the hypocrites *are*: for they love to pray standing in the synagogues and in the corners of the streets, that they may be seen of men. Verily I say unto you, They have their reward. **6** But thou, when thou prayest, enter into thy closet, and when thou hast shut thy door, pray to thy Father which is in secret; and thy Father which seeth in secret shall reward thee openly. **7** But when ye pray, use not vain repetitions, as the heathen *do*: for they think that they shall be heard for their much speaking.

When Jesus says **"inter into thy closet"** he is simply saying to you......to go someplace private, which in many cases may very well be a closet. And if you're not sure of what you would like to say, then Jesus has given us an **"example prayer"** to use, but you don't have to use it, he is just making the point that your prayer should be along these lines, which is why he says to pray: (**After this manner**) as shown in the verse below:

Matthew 6: (KJV)

9 After this manner therefore pray ye: Our Father which art in heaven, Hallowed be thy name. **10** Thy kingdom come. Thy will be done in earth, as *it is* in heaven. **11** Give us this day our daily bread. **12** And forgive us our debts, as we forgive our debtors. **13**

And lead us not into temptation, but deliver us
from evil: For thine is the kingdom, and the power,
and the glory, for ever. Amen.

So once again, the point that Jesus is making when
he says to pray: (**After this manner**) is that you
should be addressing God as our Father, and
acknowledging him as Holly, and you should also
show support and submission in his will being done.
You should be asking and thanking him for your
daily needs, as well as asking for forgiveness for
those whom you have hurt or wronged, and
forgiving those who have wronged or hurt you. You
should also be praying not to be tempted to do
things that are against his word (**The Bible**)....*(and
considering what this book is about, I think you
know where this applies to you*), and finally, your
prayer should include a request to be protected from
those who are evil. Then of course you end the
prayer with (**Amen**), which is a Hebrew word that
means (*Truly or Surely*), it simply means that
"you're sincere".

"*Do not*" concern yourself with any other examples
that mankind may suggest, because Jesus has
spoken!
And Jesus is and has the final word on
righteousness.................

Matthew 6: (KJV)

4 For Christ *is* the end of the law for righteousness to every one that believeth.

But be aware, that many fake preachers, false prophets and individuals have twisted the verse above to teach that Jesus did away with laws of righteousness; and that all you have to do is have faith and believe and you're no longer bound by any laws, and many people will resort to such teachings in an attempt to deceive you, while others are just plain ignorant, and like the idea of not having any laws.

But pay very close attention to the verse above, it says: (**Christ *is* the end of the law**) it doesn't say (**Christ ended the law**), there's a big difference! *"I must remind you once again of what we learned earlier in....***Chapter Two***"* about the rearrangement of words, and how it can change a message dramatically, after all, this is why I only recommend the (**King James Version**) or (**KJV**).

So when it says "**Christ *is* the end of the law**" it just means that he has the final word!

Look at it this way: if I'm serving a line of people, and I say to you "**you're the end of the line**", it doesn't mean that the line no longer exists; it just means that you're the last person, the final customer, and no one can come behind you!

145

However, it doesn't surprise me that the unrighteous would see it the other way around, and would love to be without laws, but we can quickly put an end to this age old deception with two simple verses from Jesus himself, as shown below:

Matthew 19: (KJV)

7 They say unto him, Why did Moses then command to give a writing of divorcement, and to put her away? 8 He saith unto them, Moses because of the hardness of your hearts suffered you to put away your wives: but from the beginning it was not so. 9 And I say unto you, Whosoever shall put away his wife, except *it be* for fornication, and shall marry another, committeth adultery: and whoso marrieth her which is put away doth commit adultery.

So Jesus states that marriage is a law from the beginning of time: "and in the beginning of time there were no divorces" but by Moses being a prophet of God's, God allowed Moses to alter this law and allow divorces out of sympathy for the people who were unhappily married and hard hearted about it, as Jesus stated: "**Moses because of the hardness of your hearts suffered you to put away your wives**". But then notice that Jesus

146

reenacts the original law and ultimately has the final say when he says: "**And I say unto you, Whosoever shall put away his wife, except it be for fornication, and shall marry another, committeth adultery: and whoso marrieth her which is put away doth commit adultery**"

So this particular verse shows that not only did Jesus "*not*" do away with any laws, but instead, he reinstated the original law, which was more binding because it limited the reasons that a person may use to get a divorce, it also shows that Jesus had "*the final say*", and could override Moses' laws, and any of the prophets laws, which means that Jesus has the "*last word*", the final say, and is: (**the end of the law**), which means that no one else can change it!

So now let's take a look at the next verse.........

Matthew 22: (KJV)

35 Then one of them, *which was* a lawyer, asked *him a question*, tempting him, and saying, **36** Master, which *is* the great commandment in the law? **37** Jesus said unto him, Thou shalt love the Lord thy God with all thy heart, and with all thy soul, and with all thy mind. **38** This is the first and great commandment. **39** And the second *is* like unto it, Thou shalt love thy neighbour as thyself. **40** On

147

these two commandments hang all the law and the prophets.

So as you can see with this verse, not only does Jesus remind them that they are under the law, but he informs them that the two new laws, embodies all of the old laws and the prophets who gave them, as he states: **"On these two commandments hang all the law and the prophets"**. So he actually broadens the law by streamlining the "**Ten Commandments**" into two major "**Commandments**", which now embodies all of the **"previous laws and the prophets who spoke them"**.
So not only are we bound to the original laws of the "**Ten Commandments**", but we are also bound by laws which you don't even see in the "**Ten Commandments**", which are laws that were spoken of by "**The prophets**", such as:

1) I **Corinthians 11:3 (KJV)** But I would have you know, that the head of every man is Christ; and the head of the woman *is* the man; and the head of Christ *is* God.

2) **Ephesians 5:11 (KJV)** And have no fellowship with the unfruitful works of darkness, but rather reprove *them.*

148

3) **Deuteronomy 22:5 (KJV)** The woman shall not wear that which pertaineth unto a man, neither shall a man put on a woman's garment: for all that do so *are* abomination unto the LORD thy God. (***Again, this is one of those laws specifically for Gays and Lesbians & Cross Dressers***)

And there are literally hundreds of laws such as these which fall under these two major commandments shown below:

1)Thou shalt love the Lord thy God with all thy heart, and with all thy soul, and with all thy mind.
2)Thou shalt love thy neighbour as thyself.

And of course we all know that a commandment is a law, RIGHT?
So knowing that, we know that commandments are all laws of righteousness, RIGHT?
It's pretty much self explanatory!
So don't allow your-self to get caught up in foolish preaching, instead, get your-self a (**KJV**) of the bible to check out what you are being told.
This particular information is profitable to all, and not just those of the Gay and Lesbian community, as there are many sins that will require God's forgiveness. However, we as individuals often think that our sins aren't as bad as the next person's, but as

the old saying goes: *"take a look at yourself before you point the finger at others"*, and that's just one of many sayings that are there to remind us that we should take a look at ourselves, before we criticize others, such as the ones listed below:

1) Why are you worrying about your neighbor's yard, when your own yard needs attending?

2) Everyone's an expert on other people's problems, but have no clue as to how to handle their own.

3) We are so conscious of the wrong that's done to us, but give no thought to the wrong we do to others.

4) **Luke 6:41(KJV)** And why beholdest thou the mote that is in thy brother's eye, but perceivest not the beam that is in thine own eye?

These are all eye-opening slogans that are there to remind us that we all have sins to be worked out, and that we should start with ourselves first before we get that self-righteous feeling.
But it doesn't mean that we should stop addressing one another's immoral and inappropriate behavior, it just means that we're not to do so with such a **"HOLLIER THAN THOU"** attitude.

And even though it's ok for us to be proud of our accomplishments, we should never become *"pride-full"* (**overly proud**), which only promotes a self-righteousness type of mentality and encourages unacceptable behavior.

The Bible describes individuals like this, who have no shame in the unrighteousness that they do, but instead are actually proud of it, and even encourages others to do so, regardless of the consequences which are to come:

Romans 1:32 (KJV)
Who knowing the judgment of God, that they which commit such things are worthy of death, not only do the same, but have pleasure in them that do them".

Such as: "**Gay and Lesbian Pride**" which promotes inappropriate behavior and encourages others to do so. This actually encourages individuals to take Pride in acts against "**God**", which seems highly unthinkable that anyone would actually say such a thing, but judging by the outpouring of support, it proves to be exactly what they're saying!
But if we take a closer look at the hype surrounding "**Gay and Lesbian Pride**", you'll find desperate individuals whom are really hurting inside, but have taken the wrong approach in being disrespectful,

rude and loud, and committing acts against God definitely isn't a reason to be proud!

But let's not kid ourselves, because every one of us commit acts against God every single day, but it's extremely rare that you will find individuals proud of doing so, and what's even more rare is finding them willing to admit to it.

However, when we commit acts against God, we can remorsefully be forgiven, which is why daily prayer is so necessary, so that we may ask for daily forgiveness, of our daily sins, but it's impossible to be remorseful when you're proud of your sin, such as "**Gay and Lesbian Pride**".

In fact, Pride suppresses remorse, because in a prideful state of mind the focus is entirely on yourself, and not the affects you have on others, and if you aren't aware of the affect you have on others, then how can there be remorse.

"So with that in mind" everyone should know that God wants all of us! Even from the lowliest of the low, to all of the rest. He doesn't want anyone left behind, "not one single person" but for this to happen, we all have to do our part, which is to repent!

I wish that I could tell you of a special pill that you could take which would remove your sins forever, but unfortunately it doesn't work that way; so instead, your "**will**" has to be that pill. Your "**will**" has to be the pill that guide you to repentance.

Even God himself will not force you to repent, because it goes against his rules of your freedom to choose, which he has given to all of mankind since the beginning of time.............

Exodus 16: (KJV)

4 Then said the LORD unto Moses, Behold, I will rain bread from heaven for you; and the people shall go out and gather a certain rate every day, that I may prove them, whether they will walk in my law, or no.

Ezekiel 14: (KJV)

6 Therefore say unto the house of Israel, Thus saith the Lord GOD; Repent, and turn *yourselves* from your idols; and turn away your faces from all your abominations.

Acts 3: (KJV)

19 Repent ye therefore, and be converted, that your sins may be blotted out, when the times of refreshing shall come from the presence of the Lord;

So none of the verses above, or any of the others in the Bible says that you have to repent, so the decision totally yours, but keep in mind that if you don' repent, then you won't be accepted by God, and the only other choice is Satan! But you should never claim pride in going against God, **"Gay and Lesbian Pride"**, even in such cases where being Gay or Lesbian may have stemmed from some legitimate trauma, such as: (child molestation, rape, etc), instead, you should always be searching for the truth.

You have to look at it this way, if you can claim pride in unrighteousness, then so can everyone else, because after all **(wrong is wrong, regardless!)** consenting or not. It all goes back to the point made earlier, that everyone thinks that their sin isn't as bad as the next's, but can you imagine a **"rapist"** feeling that exact same way, and saying: (*I was born this way and I'm proud of it*), and how about **"pedophiles"** that would say we were born this way, and then chant: (*Pedophilia Pride*), or what if **"alcoholics"** were demanding special (*alcoholic's rights?*)

Under this logic, even those who have oppressed and committed heinous acts against you would be protected, which would allow them rights just like you. Even an alcoholic would have rights that would protect them to work in factories operating dangerous machinery, or even vehicles such as cars, busses, and aircrafts, and maybe even carry firearms, which would endanger us all, because after all, *"they were born this way"*, or *"it's a*

disease", and therefore not their fault, so how then can you discriminate "*right*?"
This "**no-fault**" excuse of society is a very immoral one, but it's so accepted by the leaders of society because it's their excuse as well.
Under this logic there would literally be no end to the legislating of perversions and immorality by this society.

And speaking of society and its immoral legislations, how about "**alcoholism**" There's a myth surrounding alcoholism which associates alcoholism with diseases, but in reality, alcoholism is nothing more than a bad habit, a social and emotional crutch that results in an addiction. It's a weak individual's way of dealing with their inadequacies in social or emotional situations.
It's usually this type of weakness that will cause a person to begin drinking in the first place, and it's that same weakness that will be the reason why they can't quit, but it's "**definitely not a disease!**"
Diseases are "**organisms, bacteria or viruses**" (*Pathogens*), that attack the biological system of any living organisms foreign of it-self, usually causing damage or destruction to the extent of needing medical attention, or fatality.
Diseases' also have the ability to migrate from host to host (**person to person/creature to creature**) typically through (*but not limited to*) physical or

airborne contact, which could never happen simply by touching or breathing the same air as an "**alcoholic**". Nor do we share some gene that possesses an "**alcoholic trait**" as some doctors would suggest. Not unless of course they're referring to the gene of (**unrighteousness**), then of course this would be true!

Read your bible (KJV) to learn what a disease is. This is why the bible cautions against drinking in the first place, and absolutely forbids "**excessive drinking**" as it relates to persons in positions of authority and morality..........

Leviticus 10: (KJV)
8 And the LORD spake unto Aaron, saying, 9 Do not drink wine nor strong drink, thou, nor thy sons with thee, when ye go into the tabernacle of the congregation, lest ye die: *it shall be* a statute for ever throughout your generations:

Proverbs 31: (KJV)
4 *It is* not for kings, O Lemuel, *it is* not for kings to drink wine; nor for princes strong drink: 5 Lest they drink, and forget the law, and pervert the judgment of any of the afflicted.

Isaiah 28: (KJV)

156

7 But they also have erred through wine, and through strong drink are out of the way; the priest and the prophet have erred through strong drink, they are swallowed up of wine, they are out of the way through strong drink; they err in vision, they stumble *in* judgment.

I Timothy 3: (KJV)

2 A bishop then must be blameless, the husband of one wife, vigilant, sober, of good behaviour, given to hospitality, apt to teach; 3 Not given to wine, no striker, not greedy of filthy lucre; but patient, not a brawler, not covetous; 8 Likewise *must* the deacons *be* grave, not doubletongued, not given to much wine, not greedy of filthy lucre; 11 Even so *must* *their* wives *be* grave, not slanderers, sober, faithful in all things.

Titus 2: (KJV)

2 That the aged men be sober, grave, temperate, sound in faith, in charity, in patience. 3 The aged women likewise, that *they be* in behaviour as becometh holiness, not false accusers, not given to much wine, teachers of good things; 4 That they may teach the young women to be sober, to love their husbands, to love their children, 6 Young men likewise exhort to be sober minded.

Hosea 4: (KJV)

11 Whoredom and wine and new wine take away the heart.

So in essence, the bible teaches that drinking in moderation is ok, but because alcohol does impair and distort a person's perception and judgment, and often results in drunkenness which leads to all types or unrighteousness, **"it would be best not to drink at all"**, which it emphasizes of those in office of a moral authoritative position, as described with Kings, Princes, Bishops and Deacons. This would also apply to those in government or any other leadership role of society as it relates to authority over the people.
It also teaches that the negative effects of drinking are subtle but serious, and is for the weak, and those whom can't deal with reality and are ready to perish....................

Proverbs: (KJV)

20:1 Wine *is* a mocker, strong drink *is* raging: and whosoever is deceived thereby is not wise.
23:29 Who hath woe? who hath sorrow? who hath contentions? who hath babbling? who hath wounds without cause? who hath redness of eyes? **30** They that tarry long at the wine; they that go to seek

mixed wine. **32** At the last it biteth like a serpent, and stingeth like an adder.

Proverbs 31: (KJV)

6 Give strong drink unto him that is ready to perish, and wine unto those that be of heavy hearts. **7** Let him drink, and forget his poverty, and remember his misery no more.

Isaiah 5: (KJV)

11 Woe unto them that rise up early in the morning, *that* they may follow strong drink; that continue until night, *till* wine inflame them!

So here you can see that the whole alcoholism thing isn't anything new, and that there were always alcoholics, and will always be alcoholics, as well as counsel against it, just as it is shown here.
But in spite of the darker side of wine and strong drinks, there were positive contributions made from them, as they were also used as a cleansing / purifying method for the body, as sort of a **"medicinal practice"**.............

Timothy 5: (KJV)

23 Drink no longer water, but use a little wine for thy stomach's sake and thine often infirmities.

But of course **"like everything else"** mankind just has to take it too far! But whatever your device or claim to unrighteousness may be, it really doesn't matter, because **"God says quit"**, and get yourself right!

This is one of the beautiful things about God and righteousness, which is to say that God **"unlike man"** doesn't except excuses, and we shouldn't look to make excuses, or seek special rights in unrighteousness.

"In fact" when you seek special rights in unrighteousness, you are actually taking the same unrighteousness that was perpetrated on you in causing your unrighteousness, and perpetuating that behavior, it's all just one big cycle of immorality. And it's the leaders of all societies on earth that permit such behavior, especially as it relates to the **"government"**, which has a strong showing of support from likeminded individuals who's rights are being protected to pervert and be perverted, such as **"Gays and Lesbians"**, whose actions are perverse in itself, *"even though they do not like to view it as such"*.

But acts of perversion are those that deviate from the natural intended purpose, which is an act that: **(Distorts, corrupt, abuse, misuse or misrepresents the appropriate course of conduct).**

Don't believe God?

Well how about the definition given from a
dictionary of your peers (A World Dictionary)
The definition given below is most commonly used
by the world, in all societies

Per·vert
Verb
Pervert

**1. Alter (something) from its original course,
meaning, or state to a distortion or
corruption of what was first intended.**
*"He was charged with conspiring to pervert the course of
justice"*

Synonyms:
distort, corrupt, subvert, twist, bend, abuse,
misapply, misuse, misrepresent, misinterpret, falsify
"People who attempt to pervert the rules"

Noun
Pervert

**1. A person whose sexual behavior is regarded
as abnormal and unacceptable.**

Synonyms: deviant, degenerate;

Informal: Perv.....Dirty old man.....Sicko......

"A Sexual Pervert"

So by all definitions, the gay and lesbian lifestyle is a perverted one, regardless of one's acknowledgement or acceptance of the facts!

So if you don't want to be a pervert, then don't practice perversion, otherwise, you cannot take offence to being seen for what you are!
And the same holds true in every aspect of life, which is to say:

*If you do not want to be a lawyer, then don't practice law.
*If you do not want to be a doctor, then don't practice medicine.
*If you do not want to be an accountant, then don't practice accounting.

"*You are what you are*" and "*it is what it is*!" In other words, the sky will not be considered purple because you have a problem with the color blue, and a lie is still a lie regardless of how many people you get to agree with you. Furthermore, the Gay and Lesbian lifestyle is a **"knock-off"** of God's intended purpose for men and women, as it mimics what God has established as the natural order for men and women, (*hence the physical structure*). So why then, when it comes to something as important

162

as your life, would you choose one that's a **"knock-off"**, especially given the fact that many of you won't even invest in a **"knock-off "**product, and your life is clearly a much bigger investment, *"so shouldn't you have the real thing?"*

The bible teaches us to be righteous, **(ladies and gentleman)** noble and full of integrity, but in today's world, **(ladies and gentleman)** are becoming more extinct, and everyone should be striving for lifestyles that are worthy of respect, but instead their only concern is with being politically correct. In fact, this generation is so void of God that most men have become either feminized or weak, and have taken to whining and complaining instead of standing on their own two feet.

Never before in the history of mankind has the entire world come together so unanimously against God, especially every nation all at once, "except in the days of Noah"....................

Genesis 6: (KJV)

5 And GOD saw that the wickedness of man *was* great in the earth, and *that* every imagination of the thoughts of his heart *was* only evil continually. **6** And it repented the LORD that he had made man on the earth, and it grieved him at his heart. **7** And the LORD said, I will destroy man whom I have

created from the face of the earth; both man, and
beast, and the creeping thing, and the fowls of the
air; for it repenteth me that I have made them. **8**
But Noah found grace in the eyes of the LORD. **9**
These *are* the generations of Noah: Noah was a just
man *and* perfect in his generations, *and* Noah
walked with God. **11** The earth also was corrupt
before God, and the earth was filled with violence.
12 And God looked upon the earth, and, behold, it
was corrupt; for all flesh had corrupted his way
upon the earth. **13** And God said unto Noah, The
end of all flesh is come before me; for the earth is
filled with violence through them; and, behold, I
will destroy them with the earth. **17** And, behold, I,
even I, do bring a flood of waters upon the earth, to
destroy all flesh, wherein *is* the breath of life, from
under heaven; *and* every thing that *is* in the earth
shall die.

So you can see that there once was a time when the
earth was filled with much of what's happening
today, in fact the verse above describes the entire
earth as being filled with violence and corruption,
and says that the thoughts of mankind were
continually evil, **"Sound familiar?"**

So Noah was not a perfect man in terms of never
having made mistakes, or not having any faults,

164

because no man has the ability to be perfect, as shown in the verse below:

Ecclesiastes 7: (KJV)

20 For *there is* not a just man upon earth, that doeth good, and sinneth not.

But the bible expresses that he was considered perfect in his generation, especially with everything that was going on, and in spite of it all he managed to maintain a just and righteous heart. But in today's world, it's highly unlikely that even (**1%**)of the world's population measures up to this standard of righteousness; a standard that simply requires seeking God with all of your heart and all of your soul, and making the effort to live by God's word (**The Bible**). But looking at the world today, it's pretty safe to say that the number of people that are actually seeking God with all of their heart and soul, is probably about (**1%**) of the world's population, and that other (**99%**) of the world's population would be those who are not making a true effort to live by God's word (**The Bible**). This is much like the days of (**Noah and Lot**), where God destroyed mankind and saved these two and their families alive because they sought God with all of their heart and all of their soul, and made the effort to live according to God's word.

165

And even though these percentages may be skewed
somewhat, the fact remains that the percentage of
those who measure up to the standard of (**Lot and
Noah**) by moral calculations, wouldn't result in
much more than (**1%**) of the world's population .
And while some may disagree, you can't dispute the
facts, so let's take a look at it from a factual stand
point, and if you find yourself in any of the
categories listed below, then you do not qualify as
one of those that make up that less than (**1%**) of the
world's population that God would save alive, as he
did with (**Lot and Noah**).

Categories:

- ✓ **Gay and Lesbian** (homosexuality).
- ✓ **Premarital Sex** (fornication).
- ✓ **Cheating Spouses** (adultery).
- ✓ **Excessive drinking** (alcoholism).
- ✓ **Racist/ Prejudice** (not loving thy neighbor
  as thyself, breaking God's commandment).
- ✓ **Lying/ Cheating/ Favoritism/ Falsifying**
  (corruption).
- ✓ **Physical or mental mistreatment of a
  Spouse** (spousal abuse) **including neglect
  and abandonment.**

- ✓ **Physical or mental mistreatment of a Child** (child abuse) **including neglect and abandonment.**
- ✓ **Stealing** (thief).
- ✓ **Self Abuse** (smoking, drugs, fighting, etc).
- ✓ **Pornography** (anything sexual, or sexually suggestive that will be practiced, viewed, worn, or listened to by individuals whom are not in a marital relationship to one another, especially clothing that will be worn in public if it has a sexually suggestive undertone, which exposes or emphasize cleavage, breasts, genitals or the buttocks region.
- ✓ **Hypocrisy/Blasphemy** (having a false devotion to God, but living as the world does by participating and accepting some or all of the above practices.

Now after taking a second look at it, it would appear that the percentage of those who measure up to the standard of (Lot and Noah), is even less than a **(1/2%)** of the world's population.

In fact, just fornication alone wipes out about 90% of the world's population as being worthy of salvation, but that doesn't mean that God won't have mercy on you depending on your situation, it just means that *"for the record"*, and all intents and purposes, *"you really aren't worthy!"*

167

And this doesn't mean that a person would have to be perfect, but we would sure have to be of a higher standard of morality than the categories listed above.

But this really isn't anything new, it's actually something that we all should have learned by the time we're full grown, especially considering that there's a Bible accessible practically everywhere you go.

And even though the churches are most often shifty and shady, and full of self-serving preachers and individuals, they too will make the mistake of telling the truth once in a while. But for the most part, those whom call themselves preachers and teachers of the gospel, regardless of their denomination, tend to preach **"not to offend"**. They will preach sermons which are known as (**FEEL GOOD SERMONS**). In other words, they will tell you that you're ok, when really you're not!

They're very careful not to offend, and risk losing your support. But true preachers and teachers of the gospel do not need your support, and have no desire to withhold the truth, nor are they at liberty of being careful not to offend.

Even Jesus taught that he did not come to spread peace on earth, but to set boundaries, so that people may choose between right and wrong, which will pit father against son and mother against daughter and families against one another.......................

Matthew 10: (KJV)

34 Think not that I am come to send peace on earth: I came not to send peace, but a sword. **35** For I am come to set a man at variance against his father, and the daughter against her mother, and the daughter in law against her mother in law. **36** And a man's foes *shall be* they of his own household.

So Jesus set the example by teaching with the truth, and not (**FEEL GOOD SERMONS**), which isn't what we see today. As a matter of fact, in today's gospel the truth is held to boundaries, while the lie is spewed freely. But the truth has no boundaries, and those who speak it are not respecters of persons, which mean that they couldn't care less about who likes and who doesn't; their only concerns are in the name of Jesus Christ!
The truth is also very powerful, and touches every emotion known to man; it also forces us to examine ourselves and our behavior, and is cleverly designed by "**God**" to work in conjunction with our conscience, which is why it is largely feared by many, actually "**by most**!" This is why the bible described (**metaphorically**) that when people choose to live immorally and accept unrighteousness, they would rather have their

conscience seared with a hot iron than to accept the truth...............

I Timothy 4: (KJV)

1 Now the Spirit speaketh expressly, that in the latter times some shall depart from the faith, giving heed to seducing spirits, and doctrines of devils; **2** Speaking lies in hypocrisy; having their conscience seared with a hot iron;

They would rather have their conscience removed because the truth stimulates the conscience, which agitates the soul, and results in emotional stress. This is why so many people will turn to mind numbing methods such as alcohol and drugs to avoid dealing with the truth, which exposes the unrighteousness in us.

So over the years there are a number of catchy phrases that evolved which were used to remind us of the significance of the truth, such as:

> ➤ **The truth hurts.**
> ➤ **The truth will set you free.**
> ➤ **Tell the truth shame the Devil.**
> ➤ **Tell the truth and the Devil will flee.**
> ➤ **You're a liar and the truth isn't in you.**

➢ **You can't handle the truth.**

These are all phrases that express the necessity of telling the truth, which many will still refuse to do even unto this day. In fact, notice that you don't see any of the so called religious denominations in the world today speaking out on the truth about the immorality of a Gay and Lesbian lifestyle. This can be attributed to the fact that there aren't any religious denominations that are **"Christ-like"**, they're all self-absorbed mammon driven institutions lead by ego stricken individuals who have no affiliation with **"Christ"**.

So let's see how many of these so called religious denominations will have something to say about the immorality of a Gay and Lesbian lifestyle after the release of this book.

"Watch for all of the false convictions of those who have said nothing up until this point"

And speaking of false convictions, did you know that many of the denominations that claim to practice (**Christianity**) actually have nothing to do with the worship of God? They're just manmade institutions full of rituals conjured up by those of past or present times to give the impression of being (**Holy**), and to satisfy the egos of those at the top of these organizations.

171

In fact, many of their practices and acts of worship are copied from the same **"pagan religions"** of biblical times which Jesus himself condemned, and specifically said **"NOT TO DO!"** As shown below:

Matthew 6: (KJV)

1 Take heed that ye do not your alms before men, to be seen of them: otherwise ye have no reward of your Father which is in heaven. **2** Therefore when thou doest *thine* alms, do not sound a trumpet before thee, as the hypocrites do in the synagogues and in the streets, that they may have glory of men. Verily I say unto you, They have their reward.
5 And when thou prayest, thou shalt not be as the hypocrites *are*: for they love to pray standing in the synagogues and in the corners of the streets, that they may be seen of men. Verily I say unto you, They have their reward.
7 But when ye pray, use not vain repetitions, as the heathen *do*: for they think that they shall be heard for their much speaking.
16 Moreover when ye fast, be not, as the hypocrites, of a sad countenance: for they disfigure their faces, that they may appear unto men to fast. Verily I say unto you, They have their reward.
17 But thou, when thou fastest, anoint thine head, and wash thy face; **18** That thou appear not unto

men to fast, but unto thy Father which is in secret: and thy Father, which seeth in secret, shall reward thee openly.

So Jesus taught that it's inappropriate to worship seeking attention, as many people like to do. And In the manor of fasting, Jesus condemns markings on the face, such as the forehead, cheeks, chin and such, so that everyone will know what you are doing. He also warned of the vanity in lengthy prayers and cleaver speech "**which God does not receive**" but instead just ends up being in vain by those whom look to be seen of others. And then of course there are those who do Alms for the entire world to see, (seeking attention).
These are all false practices, which goes directly against the **(teachings of Christ)**.
Jesus further describes some of the false practices and forbidden titles used among those of biblical times whom claimed to represent the gospel, and even though Jesus forbids the use of such titles and practices, there are many religions today who's leaders continue to defy Jesus with such behavior, by referring to themselves using these titles and continuing these practices........

Matthew 23: (KJV)

1 Then spake Jesus to the multitude, and to his disciples,

5 But all their works they do for to be seen of men: they make broad their phylacteries, and enlarge the borders of their garments, **6** And love the uppermost rooms at feasts, and the chief seats in the synagogues, **7** And greetings in the markets, and to be called of men, Rabbi, Rabbi. **8** But be not ye called Rabbi: for one is your Master, *even* Christ; and all ye are brethren. **9**   And call no *man* your father upon the earth: for one is your Father, which is in heaven. **10** Neither be ye called masters: for one is your Master, *even* Christ.

So Jesus explains that (**Rabbi, Master and Father**) are not to be used by anyone as it relates to **"Christianity or Moral Authority**!" He explains that the only one worthy of such a title is **"God"**, and that all men are **"brethren"** (equal in Christianity). This means that no one should be using these titles, **"NO ONE!"** And anyone who does is violating Jesus' authority, and therefore **"DOES NOT"**....represent him!

Furthermore, to refer to yourself or anyone else as such, only suggests that this individual is equal to God, because Jesus says that even he himself isn't worthy of such a title, and that only one is, which is his Father (**God**) who is in heaven.

However, the title "**Father**" is permitted in a domestic parental setting, whether it's biological or otherwise, but never in a "**Christian, Moral, or Authoritative setting**".

Many people have been mislead by those claiming to be of Christ, which has had its share of impact in the rise of the Gay and Lesbian community, so even though this book was written to enlighten those of the Gay and Lesbian community, "*It speaks to everyone*", because every aspect of life has had some sort of contribution to the manipulation and abuse of individuals, (**either as children or adults**), into the Gay and Lesbian lifestyle, which starts at the very top with the unrighteous immoral acts of politicians who endorse and legislate such acts, right down to the individuals and their family members who support them.

And as for those in support of the "**Gay and Lesbian**" lifestyle, you really need to find out what God has to say about it, and forget about what (**society, the government, and family members and friends**) have to say, because (**ETERNAL DAMNATION**) awaits all who defy God.

So before you get to comfortable with those rights of yours that the government protect so well, you need to understand that all they've really done is secured your place in Hell.

175

And believe it or not, women are by far the biggest supporters of the Gay and Lesbian community, which really shouldn't be too suppressing when you consider the fact that sin entered into the world by way of a woman.

"Remember", it was the woman who first sinned, and enticed the man to do the same. In fact, man was created first, but it was the woman who first sinned, which introduced it to the world. This has lead to women being blamed for the decline of the world. This has also sparked many slogans, such as: **(the Devil has a vagina)** which implies that women are the root cause behind all of the evil in the world. But even though sin entered the world through a woman, the fact of the matter is: *"Satan will work with anyone who's willing to work with him"*. Women have also been accused of being worse than men when it comes to being deceptive, which is characteristic of Satan's, but the reality of such a statement can never really be known, however, many women have really shown support for" **unrighteous - immoral**" behavior.

And Satan has certainly made a point in using women well, especially for their lewd and provocative behavior, which is evident in every aspect of life, but most notably the music and entertainment industry, where most are willing to do just about anything, no matter how immoral or inappropriate the behavior, and sadly most of them

176

are mothers of impressionable children, whose lives are subsequently being ruined. And it's the impressionable years of a child's life where training is most important, as it will become a child's foundation forever:

Proverbs 22: (KJV)

6 Train up a child in the way he should go: and when he is old, he will not depart from it.

And likewise, it can also be said:

"Train-up a child in the way he shouldn't go and he may not depart from it as well"

This is why so many people are accustomed to immorality, "*they lack proper training*".
You may have heard it said "**it takes a village to raise a child**" but actually, nothing could be further from the truth, because this would have to be either **"a very dumb village, or one very dumb child"**, especially since children are apt to learn and eager to please.
Besides, children have no power or authority over the adults, and in no way are they wiser than adults, so those who find it monumentally challenging when it comes to raising children, simply aren't following biblical teachings, and are more than likely using methods of society's, which would

177

indeed make it a monumental task. So in short, the parents just aren't living up to the task.

In fact, Parents have abandoned their God given responsibility to the children in exchange for the lusts of the world, and have detached themselves from their respective roles as parents, and their assignments as adults.

For example: women are the head of the children, and are therefore responsible for their up-bringing, and as women and mothers, should never encourage males or females to be less than their intended purpose, such as (**Gay or Lesbian**) which isn't a nurturing role, especially since women were created nurturers, and one through whom life is given.

And as (**wives**), women are to be as one with their husbands, fighting the good fight, (**the fight of righteousness**), and eschewing all ungodliness, evil and worldly lusts. And of course as "**mothers**", they are gravely responsible for the children, "*to see to it*"....that they are loved, nurtured, and protected, leaving nothing undone that will give justifiable cause to those who would chide against them in the wake of a child's rebellion.

But the correction of children is becoming scarcer every day, and as a matter of fact, women are typically supportive of even the most rebellious child, which is why so many children have been raised to think that (**homosexually**) is ok. In fact, women comparably to men are far more supporting of Gays and Lesbians, and also outnumber Gay men by a landslide as (**Lesbians**). And "believe it or not", most men seem to think that it's ok for a woman to be a Lesbian, verses a man being Gay. But once again nothing could be farther from the truth, because perversion is perversion, "*regardless of who's doing it!*"

But the reason most heterosexual men are accepting of the Lesbian lifestyle is because they don't believe it affects their morals, especially if they aren't accepting of Gay men. They will actually disassociate themselves as being (**perverted**) by rationalizing that it is the Lesbian's perversion, and it is they, who are "*crossing boundaries*", therefore as men, what fault is it of theirs for being accepting?

But the reality of it all is as with any sin, which is to say:" **acceptance makes you just as guilty as participating**", especially as far as God is concerned, so the moral disassociation used by men in this scenario "**won't work**" with God. Furthermore, the acceptance of Lesbians is equivalent to the acceptance of Gay men, the only difference is gender; but the sin is exactly the same.

For example, it would be like saying:

- I only discriminate against men and not women.

179

- I steal from elderly women, but not elderly men.
- I cheat little girls, not little boys.
- I only commit crimes with women, not men.

In all of the examples given above, (**gender**) is the only difference, but all of them are sin.

So just because you're selective of the gender, it doesn't make it any less of a sin.

But people are often very crafty when rationalizing their sins, and will stop at almost nothing when making excuses for them.

It's extremely rare that an individual will receive God's word (**The Bible**), and admit that they need to change". In fact, just mentioning someone's sin will have them fighting you tooth and nail trying to defend it. Sin can be very deceptive, especially since it's initiated by Satan, (**the master of deception**) whom knows all of your desires, and the foolishness of your heart, whom lures with the promise of glory in exchange for acts of sin. But God gives glory freely just out obedience.

Jesus is the perfect example of this as Satan tried to tempt him to sin:

Luke 4: (KJV)

1 And Jesus being full of the Holy Ghost returned
from Jordan, and was led by the Spirit into the
wilderness, **2** Being forty days tempted of the devil.
And in those days he did eat nothing: and when
they were ended, he afterward hungered. **3** And
the devil said unto him, If thou be the Son of God,
command this stone that it be made bread. **4** And
Jesus answered him, saying, It is written, That man
shall not live by bread alone, but by every word of
God. **5** And the devil, taking him up into an high
mountain, shewed unto him all the kingdoms of
the world in a moment of time. **6** And the devil
said unto him, All this power will I give thee, and
the glory of them: for that is delivered unto me;
and to whomsoever I will I give it. **7** If thou
therefore wilt worship me, all shall be thine. **8** And
Jesus answered and said unto him, Get thee behind
me, Satan: for it is written, Thou shalt worship the
Lord thy God, and him only shalt thou serve. **9**
And he brought him to Jerusalem, and set him on a
pinnacle of the temple, and said unto him, If thou
be the Son of God, cast thyself down from hence: **10**
For it is written, He shall give his angels charge
over thee, to keep thee: **11** And in *their* hands they
shall bear thee up, lest at any time thou dash thy
foot against a stone. **12** And Jesus answering said
unto him, It is said, Thou shalt not tempt the Lord

thy God. **13** And when the devil had ended all the temptation, he departed from him for a season.

So we see here that everything that Satan tried to tempt Jesus with, he already had, due to the fact that he's the son of God whom controls everything, but never the less, Satan tried to present these things to Jesus as if they were his to give, but Jesus was on an assignment from God which did not involve seeking possessions of the world, so even if Satan could have given Jesus those things, Jesus would not have accepted them. But Satan thought that he could take advantage of Jesus when he saw him hungry and weak from fasting, he thought that he would catch Jesus with his guard down and deceive him into disobeying God.

And this is exactly what Satan does with us every day in many different ways, from the subtlest of suggestions, to the most outright blunt demands. For example: notice in the verses above how subtle Satan is in his approach with Jesus when he tries to tempt him to change a stone into bread, He tries to tempt Jesus with something that he knows he need, seeing that he had just come out of a **(forty day)** fast, and was probably pretty hungry. But even then Jesus didn't allow himself to be tempted beyond God's word, which means that he had to ignore his desire **(to eat)** and put God first! Also notice how blunt Satan can be: as he suggests to Jesus to throw himself off of the temple, and states that God will save him *"if he is in fact the son of God?"* but once again, Jesus resists temptation, and obeys God. These are all examples that we are suppose to follow, *"which many of you will never do"*, because you will never look past your own desires, and put God first!

This is exactly what Satan has done with the introduction of (**Homosexuality**), he has suggested to you the (**Gay and Lesbian**) lifestyle, and you've accepted...."**Hook, Line, and Sinker**", which is the absolute same power of suggestion that he used with Jesus, the only difference is that Jesus was tempted with a much harder choice, because he was tempted with a real need...(**Food)**, especially since he could have very easily turned a stone into bread, but he resisted temptation, which couldn't have been an easy thing to do while starving. In fact, how many times have you been hungry "**absolutely starving**" with the ability to get something to eat, but denied yourself? And it's a proven fact that if you don't eat, "**you will die!**"

Food is an absolute "**requirement**" to live, unlike (**Homosexuality**), whereas if you were to quit today, you *absolutely positively* "**will not die**", but just like Adam and Eve (**Gays and Lesbians**) have chosen to follow Satan instead of God.

The (**Gay and Lesbian**) lifestyle was established by Satan. He knew that by offering an alternative to that which God has established, he could disrupt God's "**Holy Union**" of man and woman with one that isn't holy, but is instead full of (sin), "HIS AGEND".

Satan knows that the glory of God comes from man, whom God created in his own image, and the glory of (Man) comes from the woman, and the (Woman's) glory come through her children.

So Satan knew that if he could disrupt God's union of the two, the woman would fail with the children, and therefore lose her glory, which would in turn cause the man to lose his glory due to the failure of the woman, and ultimately rob God of his glory due to the failure of the man.

So as you can see, Satan had a very clever plan, because his introduction of "**homosexuality**" has spread all throughout the world, but as for replacing the union of man and woman, it's a very poor alternative, because "**Lesbians**" will never be able to reproduce without the assistance of a man, and the same is true for "**Gay men**", they will never be able to reproduce without assistance of a woman, which reverts right back to God's system of things.

So even though "**Gays and Lesbians**" have bowed down to Satan's command, they still mimic God's establishment of man and woman, which is why the men will act feminine (*like women*) and the women will act masculine (*like men*), and both absolutely need God's system of reproduction if even they are

184

to continue the legacy of "**homosexuality**" here on earth, because not even Satan can help them with that!

Furthermore, the union of a man and woman is far more glorious and gratifying than anything ever even imaginable by those of the "**Gay and Lesbian**" community, and it was established by God, whom offers "*no substitutes!*" In fact, Only Satan offers alternatives to that which God has established, which is self-explanatory....and stands to reason.

Also, as a "**Gay or Lesbian**" individual it is impossible to experience true love or intimacy, which is "*pure in nature and clean in spirit*", which just happens to be the (**oracle**) of love, and is un-achievable outside of these boundaries, "*even as a heterosexual*", but definitely not as homosexuals.

And here's why………

When "**Gays and Lesbians**" attempt acts of intimacy there's a redundant transfer of emotions, such as: (**male to male and female to female**) which can never be reciprocated properly.

It's a very artificial (**partnership/union**), in which neither is genetically capable of the necessary stimulation and growth, which are essential in the capacity of prudent mental health and wellness, and is imperative of intimate continuity. Nor are they

185

physically or genetically capable to meet and
receive one another in the appropriate orientation
which heterosexuals are designed to do.
So therefore, as **"Gays and Lesbians"**, an
individual is totally incapable of the appropriate
stimulation which allows for a true spiritual
communication due to their inappropriate
orientation. And it is during these encounters of
men and women where true spiritual
communication begins.
So at the very moment of **"intimacy"** the
communication begins, in which our bodies connect
perfectly to transmit and receive signals about one
another through physical contact and stimulation,
which initiates spiritual communication, a process
totally unique to **"Heterosexuals"**, and impossible
to achieve as **"Homosexuals"**, whom posses the
exact same physical limitations which makes it
impossible for this kind of communication.
This is also why there is such a strong bond
between men and women during intimacy, as it is
the natural act of communicating love spiritually,
and any other acts of intimacy outside of this
anatomy, only equates to (**substandard sex**), which
gives the illusion of being adequate due to the
physical stimulation. And believe it or not, even
substandard sex has led many to believe that they're
in love, at least until they're forced to live with one
another. But make no mistake about it, only a

woman complement a man's spirit, just as a man does with hers.

Furthermore, heterosexuals can communicate in ways intimately that are impossible for Gays and Lesbians, which are exclusive to heterosexuals due to their genetic capabilities, and there's so much more that takes place during intimacy than just two bodies coming together physically.

In fact, during these acts of intimacy women can actually be inspired of men to ovulate, or sustain ovulation, which will result in the woman's biological preparation for reproduction. Likewise, men can be equally inspired of women to produce significant amounts of semen, which will ensure fertilization, also resulting in reproduction. It is during these acts of intimacy that information is exchanged about one another, which maximizes the experience and intensifies the pleasure.

But this level of ecstasy requires both male and female energy, which cannot be achieved through same sex acts of intimacy, such as males (**positive**) or just females (**negative**). It's much like the flow of electricity that illuminates a light, which means that you will never get electricity to flow with just two of the same energies; it will always require both (**negative and positive**) charges, which will **"illuminate, or lighten"**.

So due to the fact that Gays lack the negative and Lesbians lack the positive, then there can be no "**light!**", and in the absence of light there's only "**darkness**", and if there is only darkness, then it is impossible to see, and the absence of sight leaves little understanding, and little understanding leads to much "**confusion!**" Hence: (**Gays and Lesbians**).

And this confusion has led many heterosexuals to ask the question: how could anyone become (**Gay or Lesbian**), when it's so obvious that males and females are purposed for each other?

"*They argue*"….that even if you find yourself in that situation, you'd have to admit that something is wrong, and quite honestly "*they're right!*"

After all let's face it, "*we all know when something is wrong!*" and here's an example : let's say you woke up tomorrow and attempt to move your right arm but the left one moved instead, so you attempt to move your left, but then the right one moved, you would know "**immediately**" that something is wrong…."*right*?" You would know that somehow throughout the night your process of transmitting signals got crossed.

Well it's no different with (**Gays and Lesbians**), which is to say that somewhere throughout life, their signals got crossed, because they're attempting to have (**Homosexual**) relationships, in a (**Heterosexual**) setting, "*in other words*" they're attempting to move their right arm, but the left is moving instead! So there are definitely some signals

188

being crossed somewhere, and it isn't in the womb, where no thoughts or desires take place, nor was it at birth. We know this because common sense dictates it, and establishes that you can't take thoughts of things of which you have no knowledge, and you can't have desires for that which does not exist. All of this is coupled with the fact that this is the developing stage of life where you have no knowledge of anything, and will have to be taught everything! "**This should be common sense**" but for those of you whom are having trouble with this fact, let's see what God has to say, as he is very clear in his teachings............

Deuteronomy: (KJV)

1:39 Moreover your little ones, which ye said should be a prey, and your children, which in that day had no knowledge between good and evil, they shall go in thither, and unto them will I give it, and they shall possess it.

31:13 And *that* their children, which have not known *any thing*, may hear, and learn to fear the LORD your God, as long as ye live in the land whither ye go over Jordan to possess it.

So just as God states in the verses above: children have no knowledge of "**good or evil**", and do not know "**Any-thing**", which includes

189

(**Heterosexuality**) or (**Homosexuality**), he even
states that they will have to be taught to know him.
So clearly, children have no knowledge base of
anything, (**in the womb or at birth**), except that
which their parents or guardians teach them.
Wouldn't you think that the manufactures' of auto
mobiles and household appliances know something
about their products and how the work? So don't
you think that the creator of Heaven and Earth
know a little something about his product
(**Mankind**) and how he works?
So that brings us back to the original question:
(**How could anyone become gay or lesbian?**), and
the truth is…."**it's the Parents**". Yes, the parents
are to blame for all of this confusion because both
mother and father are responsible for raising the
children, and although it's the mother whom is the
primary caregiver and the first point of contact for
the child as God has established it, the father is still
responsible for his role in raising the children, even
though his larger responsibility is to the wife. His
priority is the wife's stability, being that she's the
primary caregiver of the children. He's responsible
for making sure that the wife has everything she
need for the assignment of rearing children, and to
assist as necessary. But it is the woman whom has
been given the assignment as primary caregiver by
God, "**which is proven by her design**", being that
women were designed for conception, and are

physically equipped to provide the necessary nutritional needs of infants after birth.

So this period in between conception to the weaning of a child takes approximately 1year and 6 months. The whole process could potentially take up to 2 years before the child is weaned and the woman is able to resume her normal role as wife and mother again, which is also to be a bonding period for both mother and child. Then of course there's the assignment of training, which is where the programming of the mind will begin, and this is the stage where you will be applying information to a vacant mind, which is similar in concept to the programming of a new computer, which means that you will be loading information.

This is a very crucial period in the process of training a child, because this will be their foundation "*for life*". It is the core foundation of information, and will be to them what is known in computer terminology as the (**root directory**), much like a computer.

You may have heard of the term (**Terrible 2's**), this terminology refers to children at 2 years of age whom have become difficult to manage. This is the perfect example of a "**poor core foundation**"....a bad "**root directory**", and as the child gets older, their need for the appropriate information will become more critical. In fact, it is the toddler years of a child that are the most critical to training, and

191

as he or she moves into the adolescent years, the affirmation of this information will be revisited. And this is where we find the answer to the question:
(How could anyone become gay or lesbian?), and the answer is: **(TRAINING):**

Proverbs 22: (KJV)
6 Train up a child in the way he should go: and when he is old, he will not depart from it.

Deuteronomy: (KJV)
4:9 Only take heed to thyself, and keep thy soul diligently, lest thou forget the things which thine eyes have seen, and lest they depart from thy heart all the days of thy life: but teach them thy sons, and thy sons' sons;
6:5 And thou shalt love the LORD thy God with all thine heart, and with all thy soul, and with all thy might. **6:6** And these words, which I command thee this day, shall be in thine heart: **6:7** And thou shalt teach them diligently unto thy children, and shalt talk of them when thou sittest in thine house, and when thou walkest by the way, and when thou liest down, and when thou risest up.

Isaiah 54: (KJV)

13 And all thy children *shall be* taught of the LORD; and great *shall be* the peace of thy children.

So once again, we see here that children do have to be trained, because all of their aspirations will depend largely on what they are taught. And even though many people would like to think that they did well in raising their children, *"the truth is in the results!"*
Also notice the emphasis that is put on the necessity of training a child, as described in the verses above, such as:

"Train up a child and he will not depart from it"
"Teach thy sons and thy son's sons"
"Teach them diligently to your children"
"Talk about it when you're at home, out and about, before bedtime, and when you wake"

So you can see the importance of training a child, and the seriousness in which it must be done. You must stay at it **"24/7"** (**24 hours a day/ 7 days a week**), otherwise, it would stand to reason why anyone would think that they were born that way: (**Gay or Lesbian**).
You cannot allow a window of opportunity for Satan, because he will deceive them into believing that homosexuality is ok, *"especially children"*, who will mimic everything that they see. In fact,

children will often mimic the behavior of their parents so closely that it has lead to many catchphrases referencing the likeness of the child to the parent.

Phrases Such as:

- Like father like son / like mother like daughter.
- The fruit doesn't fall far from the tree (which means children will reflect their parents).
- He/she got it honest (this describes a child whose behavior mimics that of the parent).
- You are your mother's daughter (this refers to a child that behaves just like the parent).

All of these catchphrases reflect the behavior of a child due their upbringing and environment, and further expresses the fact that parents are the primary influence over their own children, which means that if the parent's behavior is inappropriate then so will the child's be, because wickedness does not produce righteousness..........

Job 14:4 (KJV) Who can bring a clean *thing* out of an unclean? not one.

The verse above also exposes how we all became sinners in the first place, being that we all come from an unclean source: (**Adam and Eve**), so if the parents make conscious choices to practice sin, then the children don't stand a chance! But realistically, there's absolutely no excuse for a child to behave inappropriately under the guidance of their parents, which means that if a child is raised morally and grows up to become immoral, in no way does this reflect on the parents who have proven to have done their job.

But if a child is raised immorally and grows up to continue the immorality, then as an adult he or she shall be held accountable for their actions, and the parents are held accountable as well, as they have proven not to have done their job while the individual was yet a child.

And the same is true for those aspiring to teach the gospel, such as: (preachers, pastors, priests and all others), they are held accountable **for what they preach or teach.**

This is also the perfect example of why there could never be a (**Gay or Lesbian**) preacher, or teacher of the Gospel (**God's word**), because God has ordained that those who teach the Gospel "**must live by the gospel!**"

1Corinthians 9:14 (KJV)

Even so hath the Lord ordained that they which preach the gospel should live of the gospel.

So how then, could a (**Gay or Lesbian**) preacher teach against homosexuality when they themselves are homosexuals? It would not be consistent with the verse above, nor is it consistent with the verses below!

Romans 2: (KJV)

21 Thou therefore which teachest another, teachest thou not thyself? thou that preachest a man should not steal, dost thou steal? **22** Thou that sayest a man should not commit adultery, dost thou commit adultery? thou that abhorrest idols, dost thou commit sacrilege?

So here's the question:
"Can thou teach that it is a sin to be (**Gay or Lesbian**) when thou thyself are Gay or Lesbian?"

Remember, "**He that teaches the gospel must live by it!**"

So to be a (**Gay or Lesbian - Preacher**) is an **oxymoron**, as there is no such acceptance in God's Kingdom (**True Christianity**).

Also, any church or building where (**Gays and Lesbians**) may congregate in an act of worship to God, "**isn't recognized by God**", because it (**Dishonors Him!**) And the whole purpose of

196

congregating and worshiping is to (**Honor God**), and what honor is it to him if you've rejected his establishment, and being created in his image? However, this isn't limited to just Gays and Lesbians, it includes all individuals who gather erroneously in the name of God. Just remember what we learned earlier:

THERE'S A RIGHT AND A WRONG WAY TO SERVE GOD, "<u>AND YOU DO NOT GET TO CHOOSE</u>"

But you do get to choose whether or not you will serve God at all, and if you do so choose, then you cannot serve God any way you want!
There's a born again way (**acceptable to God**), and a worldly way (**unacceptable to God**).
In fact, the bible teaches us that God turns away from the wicked and the unrighteous, and "**doesn't even listen to their prayers**"

Proverbs: (KJV)
15:29 The LORD *is* far from the wicked: but he heareth the prayer of the righteous.
28:9 He that turneth away his ear from hearing the law, even his prayer *shall be* abomination.

Isaiah: (KJV)
1:15 And when ye spread forth your hands, I will hide mine eyes from you: yea, when ye make many

prayers, I will not hear: your hands are full of blood.

59:1 Behold, the LORD'S hand is not shortened, that it cannot save; neither his ear heavy, that it cannot hear: **2** But your iniquities have separated between you and your God, and your sins have hid *his* face from you, that he will not hear. **3** For your hands are defiled with blood, and your fingers with iniquity; your lips have spoken lies, your tongue hath muttered perverseness.

All of these verses above describe mostly everyone on earth, except those who have repented and changed their lives.
But now keep in mind that the parents are responsible for the children, so if you the parent **"don't have a prayer"**, then what hope is there for your children.
People often ask the question **"why does God allow bad things to happen to little children?"** which sounds like a very good question to ask, but it indicts the wrong source, which is something you'd already know had you taken the time to open a Bible!
But the more appropriate question should be" **why do parents allow bad things to happen to little children?"** this would be the more appropriate question, due to the fact that God has placed children as the responsibility of the parents, and he

did not give parents or adults responsibility over children just to have them throw it back on him. And no child was ever supposed to suffer any **(physical, mental, emotional, sexual, or biological)** abuse as the responsibility of parents or adults, which is the grossest form of negligence and abuse by parents and adults that has been perpetrated on children.

So parents and adults are responsible for the children, even right down to the many deformities and diseases' that plague children every day as a result of the parents inappropriate behavior, but even that can be overcome by prayer, provided **"they had a prayer"**, but then of course that would require that they live righteous enough to be heard, which we all know isn't going to happen!

This is why so many people today, such as **(atheists and agnostics)** will tell you that prayer doesn't work **"as if they've ever lived righteous enough to know!"** However, it's a very true saying, that if you are living unrighteous and immoral, **"You don't have a prayer"**.

This is also why it is very important that you watch your associations, to make certain that you aren't condoning or participating in any acts of immorality, which will only bring God's wrath down on you! But keep in mind that just because you have chosen to live righteously, not everyone will be accepting, because those who live unrighteous will always accuse you of being judgmental, in an attempt to divert the blame back on you, much like Gays and Lesbians have done with accusing anyone who isn't accepting of their behavior as being "**homophobic**", but that's just because they don't want you to reprove, or disassociate yourselves from them.

After all, (**Homophobic**) is just one of those vain words that the bible warns us of when it says: "**let no man deceive you with vain words**", because in this case homophobic doesn't mean: (**fear of homosexuality**), but instead (**un-accepting of it**), in which case "**true Christians**" proudly and openly agree!

So the bible warns "**watch your associations**"

Ephesians 5: (KJV)

6 Let no man deceive you with vain words: for because of these things cometh the wrath of God upon the children of disobedience. **7** Be not ye therefore partakers with them. **8** For ye were sometimes darkness, but now *are ye* light in the Lord: walk as children of light: **9** (For the fruit of the Spirit *is* in all goodness and righteousness and truth;) **10** Proving what is acceptable unto the Lord. **11** And have no fellowship with the unfruitful works of darkness, but rather reprove *them*.

"Ephesians 5:11" above states: not to have any (**fellowship**) with the unrighteous; and even further instructs you to "**reprove**" them. Now when it says "**have no fellowship**", it doesn't mean that you can't....speak to them....work with them, or even be polite to them, because you will have to communicate with them in order to reprove them, and of course as a Christian, or potential Christian, you should always show everyone respect, but what it does mean is that you are not to have them in your circle, which means as "**close friends or associates**", or even as "**residents or guest**" in your home or dwellings. And this isn't limited to just Gays and Lesbians, but should include all of those who have chosen "**unrighteousness**" as a way of life.

But this is not to confuse those who "**make unrighteous mistakes**" with those who have literally chosen unrighteousness as "**a way of life**", there's a big difference!

But also keep in mind that none of us are perfect, and everyone (**including you**) sins in some way every day, "**regardless of how righteous you may think you are**". Remember what the bible teaches us........................

Ecclesiastes 7: (KJV)

20 For *there is* not a just man upon earth, that doeth good, and sinneth not.

So this doesn't mean that if someone sins in error, or makes an honest mistake, that you can't associate with them, because if that were the case, then you couldn't associate with anyone, and there wouldn't be anyone who could associate with you due to your sins, but what this means is that if someone is making an effort to live righteously, it is then acceptable to fellowship with this person, because they have not chosen to practice sin, and are in fact making an effort to correct themselves. **"This is totally acceptable to God"** and is exactly what he wants us to do!

So even though we're born in sin, sinning doesn't have to be in us. This is where the freedom of choice comes into play and defines the difference. For example, everyone and anyone who has ever lived was born into sin as heirs, which means that your parents were sinners, and their parents were sinners, and so on, all the way back to Adam and Eve.

Remember what the bible teaches us, **"Who can bring a clean thing out of an unclean"**.......

Job 14:4 (KJV) Who can bring a clean *thing* out of an unclean? not one.

Therefore we are all heirs to our ancestor's sins.

But there's a difference between a **"born sinner"**
and a **"practicing sinner"**, and the difference is that
a **"born sinner"** is anyone who has ever lived,
which means that all of mankind are **"born
sinners"**. It's something that we're born into
through heredity, it isn't your fault, and there's
literally nothing you can do about it, and that's just
the way it is! But a **"practicing sinner"** is anyone
who chooses to sin deliberately, <u>of freewill</u>. And the
term (**Freewill**) is the operative word in the life of a
"practicing sinner", and should be "*noted*" because
it is extremely relative to the fact that everyone has
a **"Freewill"** to choose, (except children), who are
totally at the mercy of the adults, and have suffered
so much at the hands of these adults who are
"practicing sinners"; But as children, or now
adults, should know that they are not in any ways
responsible for the (**negligence, abuse, or
manipulation**), that they have suffered at the hands
of adults, nor should they feel any (**indignity,
despair or anguish**) over any situation in which
they have suffered. In fact, any memories associated
with such acts or behavior of adults should be put
aside into a (**suspended issue status**). And this
"suspended issue status" is where you should place
all of those memories of your past physical or
mental traumas which you may have suffered as the
result of the adults or peers who chose to be
"sinners".

And the whole purpose of this **"suspended issue status"** is to remove these memories from your day to day thinking so that you may move forward with your life free of any distractions associated with those memories.

But this by no means, in any **"way, shape, or form"** excuse the behavior of those responsible of such acts, nor does it belittle the seriousness in which they will be held "**accountable**", but more importantly, everything in this **"suspended issue status"** belongs to God. "That's right" the whole purpose of suspending it is to remove it from you and give it to God, because God wants all of your burdens, and it is he whom wants' to execute **(punishment/vengeance)** on those who have wrong you, **"especially the parents"**..........

I Timothy 5:8 (KJV) But if any provide not for his own, and specially for those of his own house, he hath denied the faith, and is worse than an infidel.

Ephesians 6:4 (KJV) And, ye fathers, provoke not your children to wrath: but bring them up in the nurture and admonition of the Lord.

Colossians 3:21 (KJV) Fathers, provoke not your children *to anger*, lest they be discouraged.

Exodus 22: (KJV) 22 Ye shall not afflict any widow, or fatherless child. 23 If thou afflict them in

any wise, and they cry at all unto me, I will surely
hear their cry;
Romans 12:19 (KJV) Dearly beloved, avenge not
yourselves, but *rather* give place unto wrath: for it
is written, Vengeance *is* mine; I will repay, saith the
Lord.

So Just as **Romans 12:19** described: "**give place
unto wrath**", which means to put the anger and
hatred aside, and be not stirred to vengeance, but
instead, let the place that you give unto wrath be the
"**suspended issue status**", which is just a matter of
reminding yourself through mental exercises to give
it over to God, and accept that he has it now. Just
remember, God knows all and sees all, and whether
you give it over to god or not, he's still going to
address it, because it's "**SIN**", and no one gets away
with sin!
The whole purpose of the "**suspended issue status**"
is for you to give it over to God, so that you can
have peace, because God gives peace to those who
put their trust in him, and by putting your trust in
him you're accepting to wait for his judgment on
them. And Besides that, God's (**judgment, wrath
and vengeance**) is far more punishing than
anything that you could ever even imagine! So let
God handle it, in fact, God's punishment is so
(**relentless and painful**) that even you will feel

sympathy for your oppressor, **(that's just how much God hates sin!)**
However, this doesn't mean that you cannot confront those who have wronged you, or even have them brought to justice, but in fact, it's your God given right to confront them if you so choose, whether it be on a personal level or a legal one. Furthermore, even Jesus himself encourages that we confront those who have wronged us:

Luke 17:3 (KJV)

Take heed to yourselves: If thy brother trespass against thee, rebuke him; and if he repent, forgive him.

Leviticus 19:17 (KJV)

Thou shalt not hate thy brother in thine heart: thou shalt in any wise rebuke thy neighbour, and not suffer sin upon him.

So notice in Luke 17:3, Jesus also says that if they repent, you should forgive them, which follows the same principle as the **"suspended issue status"**, but with a few exceptions. And one of those exceptions with forgiveness is that the individuals **"must repent"**, as Jesus stated: **"(if) he repent, forgive him"**, this is extremely important, because if they do not repent, then there's nothing to forgiven since they have not shown remorse. However, when a person truly repents there will be a sincere showing of remorse, as well as an effort to change.

"Repentance", is one's willingness to admit that he or she has made a mistake, and are willing to accept responsibility for their actions, and the consequence/punishment that follows, because without these two components, there is no repentance.

Never the less, **"Forgiveness"** is simply a matter of removing the hatred from your heart, and not holding a grudge, but in no way does it excuse the behavior of those who commit such acts as: (**rape, abuse, molestation, or perversion**), or any other acts of sin, nor does it exempt anyone of punishment for such acts.

So contrary to what people would like to believe, **"Forgiveness"** does not free the guilty, but instead, it **"frees the victims"**, and as for the guilty, **"punishment always follows"**, which God has established in his word, as shown in the verses below:

Ezekiel 44: (KJV)

12 Because they ministered unto them before their idols, and caused the house of Israel to fall into iniquity; therefore have I lifted up mine hand against them, saith the Lord GOD, and they shall

207

bear their iniquity. **13** And they shall not come near unto me, to do the office of a priest unto me, nor to come near to any of my holy things, in the most holy *place*: but they shall bear their shame, and their abominations which they have committed. **14** But I will make them keepers of the charge of the house, for all the service thereof, and for all that shall be done therein. **15** But the priests the Levites, the sons of Zadok, that kept the charge of my sanctuary when the children of Israel went astray from me, they shall come near to me to minister unto me, and they shall stand before me to offer unto me the fat and the blood, saith the Lord GOD: **16** They shall enter into my sanctuary, and they shall come near to my table, to minister unto me, and they shall keep my charge.

In the verses above, you can see that those who did not obey God were punished, as God stated: "**I lifted up mine hand against them and they shall bear their iniquity**", and as punishment, they were not allowed to be **(priest, preach, or hold any office in the sanctuary)**, because these were all things that are near to God as "**Holy**".
And God continued by saying: "**neither are they to come near to any of my holy things**".
So because of this, they were forced to live in the **(deplorable conditions)** in which they created, as

stated: (*they shall bear their iniquity, shame and abominations which they have committed*). But God was also forgiving, and as they repented, his forgiveness did allow them to participate in the sanctuary to maintain it, but as **"servants only"**. And as for all of those who were obedient to God, they were blessed with just the opposite, to be: **(priest, to teach, and hold offices of the sanctuary)**, and to be near to God and all that is "**Holy**" unto him.

Now in this next example, God also shows us that even though he forgives, punishment follows:

2 Samuel 12: (KJV)

9 Wherefore hast thou despised the commandment of the LORD, to do evil in his sight? thou hast killed Uriah the Hittite with the sword, and hast taken his wife *to be* thy wife, and hast slain him with the sword of the children of Ammon. **10** Now therefore the sword shall never depart from thine house; because thou hast despised me, and hast taken the wife of Uriah the Hittite to be thy wife. **12** For thou didst *it* secretly: but I will do this thing before all Israel, and before the sun. **13** And David said unto Nathan, I have sinned against the LORD. And Nathan said unto David, The LORD also hath put away thy sin; thou shalt not die. **14** Howbeit, because by this deed thou hast given great occasion to the enemies of the LORD to blaspheme, the child also *that is* born unto thee shall surely die. **15** And Nathan departed unto his house. And the LORD struck the child that Uriah's wife bare unto David, and it was very sick. **18** And it came to pass on the seventh day, that the child died. And the servants of David feared to tell him that the child was dead: for they said, Behold, while the child was yet alive, we spake unto him, and he would not hearken unto our voice: how will he then vex himself, if we tell him that the child is dead? **19** But when David saw that his servants whispered, David perceived that the child was dead: therefore David said unto his servants, Is the child dead? And they said, He is dead.

So here we learn, that God will even punish those whom he has **"chosen and ordained"**, if they are disobedient and become immoral, just as he did with Adam and Eve. In fact, even more so because they disgrace him, especially since he has taken pride in them as his representation.
So by disgracing his **"Holy"** name, they cause God to appear weak or flawed, and void of integrity for having chose them.
This example was shown in the verses above, which first shows that God forgave David by sparing him

210

his life, and putting his sin away and allowing him
to continue to live, which is reiterated here:
**"And Nathan said unto David, The LORD also
hath put away thy sin; thou shalt not die"**.
Then we see that God's mercy is followed up with
punishment to David for his iniquity and disgraceful
behavior towards God, as shown below:
**"Howbeit, because by this deed thou hast given
great occasion to the enemies of the LORD to
blaspheme, the child also *that is* born unto thee
shall surely die"**.
So you can see here that even though David was
forgiven, there was still a harsh punishment that
would follow, and not only that, but an even harsher
punishment was given to David when God stated
that from that day forward there would always be
death and destruction in David's life, which he
emphasizes here: **"Now therefore the sword shall
never depart from thine house; because thou
hast despised me"**.
So here we learn that just because God forgives
you, doesn't mean that your punishment will be
wiped away, it simply means that he may be
merciful in his discipline of you, and God shows no
favoritism in his discipline, "**just mercy**". After all,
Remember David was one of God's chosen, as
shown in this verse: **(2 Samuel 12:7 And Nathan
said to David, Thou *art* the man. Thus saith the
LORD God of Israel, I anointed thee king over**

Israel, and I delivered thee out of the hand of Saul;) so even though David was "**chosen and anointed**", his punishment was still to be harsh in pain and suffering, (and keep in mind), "**that was with mercy!**". So if God is that firm with those whom he has "**chosen and anointed**", imagine how much more so he will be with those whom he hasn't. And as sure as God has given parents charge over the children, it is up to them **both** to maintain a safe and healthy environment, regardless of their secular choices and interests.

And whether they're "**separated or divorced, local or abroad**", **both** are gravely responsible for the lives that they bring into this world, with "**no exceptions**" and "**no excuses!**"

I Timothy 5:8 (KJV) But if any provide not for his own, and specially for those of his own house, he hath denied the faith, and is worse than an infidel.

II Corinthians 12:14 (KJV) Behold, the third time I am ready to come to you; and I will not be burdensome to you: for I seek not yours, but you: for the children ought not to lay up for the parents, but the parents for the children.

So just to be clear.....**I Timothy 5:8** above; is referring to any man that has a (**wife/family**), or any children that he brings into this world.

212

And....**II Corinthians 12:14** establishes, that it is
the responsibility of (**both parents**) to provide for
the children.

So there are no "**exceptions**" and no "**excuses**",
especially considering that God's grace is sufficient
for us to accomplish whatever it is that we need to
accomplish, specifically raising children. And God's
grace was sufficient enough to provide a book of
knowledge and wisdom for us to get it done.
Therefore, it's your own fault if you mismanage
God's grace.
So due to the fact that God crated women bearers
and nurturer of children, makes them very
influential in the lives of men, which begins with
infant boys. In fact, there isn't a man alive, or one
who has ever lived (*with the exception of Adam*)
that didn't get here by way of a woman.
So every man alive or whom has ever lived would
not even exist had it not been for a woman. This is
an enormous responsibility that lies with the
women, but sadly, it isn't always received by
women that way. Never the less, women are in a
very unique position to make a positive impact in
the world as the first point of contact and nurturer of
children, but unfortunately, they themselves are so
preoccupied with their own quest for attention, that
the children end up suffering, and will often have to
fend for themselves, which leaves them exposed to

213

the world, and vulnerable to all of its attention, such as:

- Homosexuality
- Alcoholism/Drugs
- Molestation
- Physical abuse
- Mental abuse
- And so much more!

These are all acts which ruins the lives of kids every single day, due to poor parenting, in which both parents are to blame. The fathers are at fault because they've dropped the ball as moral **"leaders and supporters"** of the family, and in many cases have abandoned family altogether. Mothers are at fault for obvious reasons: (**poor rearing and nurturing**). So contrary to the purpose of a woman, many are found to be much less than virtuous when it comes to morality, which just happens to be consistent with the findings in past history.
Even Solomon, whom was the wisest man on earth, as God had blessed him to be, in searching the matters of life learned and taught many things, and one of the things he thought more specifically, is that finding a righteous man is a very hard thing, but what he found next was even harder to believe, because finding a righteous woman is nearly impossible to achieve..........

Ecclesiastes 7: (KJV)

25 I applied mine heart to know, and to search, and to seek out wisdom, and the reason *of things*, and to know the wickedness of folly, even of foolishness *and* madness: **26** And I find more bitter than death the woman, whose heart *is* snares and nets, *and* her hands *as* bands: whoso pleaseth God shall escape from her; but the sinner shall be taken by her. **27** Behold, this have I found, saith the preacher, *counting* one by one, to find out the account: **28** Which yet my soul seeketh, but I find not: one man among a thousand have I found; but a woman among all those have I not found.

So here Solomon explains that out of a thousand men, only one **"righteous"** man was found, as he states: *"one man among a thousand have I found"*. But out of that same number of women, he states that not even one **"righteous"** woman could be found:" *but a woman among all those have I not found"*.

This is eerily consistent with the findings of this book. In fact, the more we explore the mater, we find that it is the women whom are breeding and supporting wicked men, such as:

- Homosexuals

215

- Corrupt (politicians, Government, Corporations, etc)
- Child Molesters (Pedophile Priest, Teachers, Fathers, Brothers, Sons, etc)
- Sex Offenders (Rapist, Perverts, etc)
- Spousal and child abusers
- Drug (Dealers, Users, Traffickers', etc)
- Alcoholics (Daily Drinker, Excessive Drinker, etc)

And that's just to name a few, but we find that women are far more tolerant and accepting of immoral behavior than men, which is the perfect example of why women can't be effective leaders men, coupled with the fact that women are very sporadic in nature, who's moods are often dictated by hormonal balances, which can trigger an array of emotions without so much as hint or a clue, and it's all a part of nature, yes we know this much is true, **(PMS, Menopause/ Post menopause)**, is what it all comes down to.

Besides, just having men as leaders has proven to be hell enough, and they don't have nearly the baggage of women, or any of that "**PMS**" stuff.

And we all know how degenerate, immoral and perverted men can be, so the last thing we need is an understanding woman by their side, instead, it will always require that decent men control and challenge wicked men. In fact, if women could

216

actually control men, there wouldn't be so many broken dysfunctional boys, who just happen to be their sons!

"So if you can't control a boy, don't even think about controlling a man"

But women will always be supportive of the wicked behavior in men, and can be particularly supportive in the behavior of Gay men, as if there were some sort of real sisterhood that exists between the two, and yet "**once again**", playing the role of (**Eve**) "*by leading men astray!*"
But as they lead these men astray, they too will have to pay, for being encouraging of the wicked behavior of men, which now puts them in a situation where they themselves face (**Eternal Damnation**), and will suffer the same judgment as those they've encouraged to sin. But since they don't believe in "**Hell**" the reality of judgment isn't real so they continue to be supportive of these men.
However, "**Damnation**" is very real, and those who dismiss God have their fates sealed, and in the end it will be too late to repent for what we did, as every head will bow, and every knee shall kneel down, and "**all will know who God is!**"
So even though no one knows the exact logistics of "**Hell**", or even if you don't believe it's real, everyone is aware of it, and its purpose and intent,

which has been strategically arranged by God so
that no one can accuse his judgment of being
flawed, when finding themselves sentenced to an
"eternity of torment".
So whether you believe it's real or not, doesn't
change the plot, because everyone knows how the
story of hell is being told, and as the story goes,
even when it's considered fictional, it's still a place
(where all of the bad people go), a place where
people are at odds, for choosing Satan over God,
and following the world down the pathway of sin,
and there won't be any relief in sight because they
refused to "***Fight The Good Fight***" and instead
chose that which was wrong over what was right.

So let's take a look at some of what God has
revealed about **"Hell"** (**Eternal Damnation**), which
is a warning to all those whom have chosen sin:

Matthew 13: (KJV)

49 So shall it be at the end of the world: the angels
shall come forth, and sever the wicked from among
the just, **50** And shall cast them into the furnace of
fire: there shall be wailing and gnashing of teeth.

Luke 13: (KJV)

23 Then said one unto him, Lord, are there few that
be saved? And he said unto them,

218

24 Strive to enter in at the strait gate: for many, I say unto you, will seek to enter in, and shall not be able. **25** When once the master of the house is risen up, and hath shut to the door, and ye begin to stand without, and to knock at the door, saying, Lord, Lord, open unto us; and he shall answer and say unto you, I know you not whence ye are:

 26 Then shall ye begin to say, We have eaten and drunk in thy presence, and thou hast taught in our streets.

27 But he shall say, I tell you, I know you not whence ye are; depart from me, all *ye* workers of iniquity. **28** There shall be weeping and gnashing of teeth, when ye shall see Abraham, and Isaac, and Jacob, and all the prophets, in the kingdom of God, and you *yourselves* thrust out.

So Jesus explains that in the end, many people will want to go to heaven but won't be allowed, because **"the door will be closed!"** as Jesus describes: (***When once the master of the house is risen up, and hath shut to the door, and ye begin to stand without, and to knock at the door, saying, Lord, Lord, open unto us; and he shall answer and say unto you, I know you not***), and the reason for this is because once God sends the angels to earth, they already have their assignments, and at that point everyone is accounted for, as either good or bad,

219

and the wheels of "**Heavenly Justice**" are already set in motion, and you...."**are out of time!**"

Also notice what happens to those who are out of time (*the wicked*), as described by Jesus:
(*the angels shall come forth, and sever the wicked from among the just, And shall cast them into the furnace of fire*).

And you do know that this "**furnace of fire**" that it speaks of, is "**Hell**" (**Eternal Damnation**) right?

So in **Matthew 13 (KJV)**, Jesus describes a furnace and fire specifically, and states that there will be "**wailing**": (*screaming, crying, groaning*), and "**gnashing**": (*grinding, gritting, cringing*) of teeth. And there's no misunderstanding that a furnace is for fire, and there's certainly no misunderstanding about what fire does, and I'm sure that we can all agree that "**screaming, crying, groaning and gnashing of teeth**" means that someone is in some serious pain.
Jesus also describes in **Luke 13 (KJV)**, that the wicked would be pleading to enter into the Kingdom of Heaven, and he will respond:" **I know you not whence ye are; depart from me, all *ye* workers of iniquity**".

So let's take a look at some of the behavior that falls under the category of **"iniquity"**, and See if any of it fits you:
(**Homosexuality, Pedophilia, Rape, Murder, Corruption, Racism, Fornication, Adultery**), and that's just to name a few, which should give you a pretty good idea of who will be (**screaming and gnashing their teeth**) in total pain.

Jesus describes all of these things to take place "**at the end of the world**", when repentance will be too late. So those who don't believe in God, or think that they can repent in the end, are in for a very rude awakening!
This is why it is extremely important that you repent while you still have a choice, because once the end is here, you won't be allowed to choose, and your destiny will be determined by your lifestyle at that time: (**Heaven or Hell**) accordingly.

So let's take a look at another revelation of "**Hell**" (**Eternal Damnation**) which God has given us:

Luke 16: (KJV)
22 And it came to pass, that the beggar died, and was carried by the angels into Abraham's bosom: the rich man also died, and was buried;
23 And in hell he lift up his eyes, being in torments, and seeth Abraham afar off, and Lazarus in his

bosom. **24** And he cried and said, Father Abraham, have mercy on me, and send Lazarus, that he may dip the tip of his finger in water, and cool my tongue; for I am tormented in this flame. **25** But Abraham said, Son, remember that thou in thy lifetime receivedst thy good things, and likewise Lazarus evil things: but now he is comforted, and thou art tormented. **26** And beside all this, between us and you there is a great gulf fixed: so that they which would pass from hence to you cannot; neither can they pass to us, that *would come* from thence. **27** Then he said, I pray thee therefore, father, that thou wouldest send him to my father's house: **28** For I have five brethren; that he may testify unto them, lest they also come into this place of torment.

29 Abraham saith unto him, They have Moses and the prophets; let them hear them. **30** And he said, Nay, father Abraham: but if one went unto them from the dead, they will repent. **31** And he said unto him, If they hear not Moses and the prophets, neither will they be persuaded, though one rose from the dead.

So in the verses above, Jesus gives us another glimpse into **"Hell"** (**Eternal Damnation**), and its purpose, by sharing a series of events that took place during the Prophet Moses' lifetime.

First, you will notice that even in "**Hell**" you will be conscious, and able to see and feel, as Jesus described with one individual who was sent to "**Hell**", but was able to see Abraham and Lazarus in heaven:
(**And in hell he lift up his eyes, and seeth Abraham afar off, and Lazarus in his bosom**).
Jesus also explains that this individual was conscious and able feel, but of course being in "**Hell**", the only feeling you'll get is "*pain!*" (**And in hell he lift up his eyes, being in torments**).
Jesus even describes the kind of pain that this individual was tormented with:
(**Father Abraham, have mercy on me, and send Lazarus, that he may dip the tip of his finger in water, and cool my tongue; for I am tormented in this flame**).
So apparently, you will have some sort of view of *Heaven* while tormenting in *Hell*.
Secondly, Jesus describes Abraham's conversation with the individual whom was in "**Hell**", stating that those in "**Hell**" will be in total torment and desperate for relief but will get none, while those in "**Heaven**" will be comforted and cared for, he also reveals that there will be a great gulf set between *Heaven* and *Hell* that will not allow those in "*Hell*"

to cross over to ***Heaven***, nor those in ***Heaven*** to cross over to ***Hell***, as shown here: (**And beside all this, between us and you there is a great gulf fixed: so that they which would pass from hence to you cannot; neither can they pass to us, that *would come* from thence**).

So even though those in hell will have some sort of view into Heaven, they still will not be able to cross over or interact with those in Heaven, and can only be seen and heard by the authorities of Heaven, as they cry out for mercy **"in vain!"**

Third and finally, Jesus shares with us some of the most important parts of the conversation that was had between Abraham and the man whom was sent to ***Hell***, as the individual pleaded with Abraham to send someone who had died to appear to his familymembers and warn them that Hell is real, believing that if they saw someone from the dead, it would convince them that Hell is real, as he stated: **"but if one went unto them from the dead, they will repent"**.

But Abraham replied: **"They have Moses and the prophets; let them hear them. If they hear not Moses and the prophets, neither will they be persuaded, though one rose from the dead"**.

So the point that Abraham was making, was that even if he would have allowed someone from the dead to appear to his family members, they would

224

have said that the person (*was never really dead*), or that it was some sort of trick or scam. And Abraham was right, because as sure as you are reading this book, you can bet that if Abraham had sent someone from the dead to the man's family members, they would have said that it was a hoax, because that's exactly where we are today, in knowing that Jesus walked the earth and taught, and yet, many people still do not believe. Even as Jesus walked the earth and was murdered, and then resurrected within the period of a week, people of that era still refused to believe, and they were even closer to the situation than we are today.

So it just goes to show you that those who are unrighteous will always look for reasons not to believe, which will always be the mindset of the unrighteous, and that's the very reason why Abraham told the man in <u>**Hell**</u>: "**if they don't believe Moses and the Prophets, then neither will they believe someone that's sent from the dead**". And besides all of this, God is not going to receive you on your terms, but instead on his, nor will you tell God under what conditions you will (**believe or not believe**). He has already set the wheels in motion thousands of years ago, before any of us were ever even thought of, and he has laid the foundation for examination of his word many years ago as well, which provides sufficient (**proof and evidence**) of his existence, so if you aren't

225

intelligent enough to receive it, **"then that's your fault"**, and you can either **accept** or **reject** it!
But in spite of much evidence, many people will still tell you that these accounts aren't real, and that Jesus is speaking of *Hell* **"hypothetically"**. But if you've ever followed the teachings Jesus', then you would know that Jesus never uses individual's names when speaking hypothetically, which is why Jesus would never have used (**Moses and Abraham's**) names in these accounts if he was speaking hypothetically, because to do so would imply that these individuals said things that they did not say, and that would make it a lie, which is far from Jesus' to do.

So always be very suspicious of those who preach or teach contrary to Biblical teachings, especially those claiming to be religious or Christians, or of God, because there are many wolves in sheep's clothing, and many false preachers and teachers of the Bible, who just love to hide behind the pure and righteous name of God, knowing that it will get you to drop your guard and allow them to take advantage of you.

In fact, you should always lower your level of trust to anyone who makes these claims, and compare their conduct to that of (Jesus Christ's), because that's what religion and Christianity is all about, to be: **"Christ like"** a (**Christian**). And even though

226

you won't be perfect, there should be a very
apparent similarity, with no deviations.

So as adults, we must work at being **"Christians"
(Christ like)**, if we are ever to be accepted in
heaven. But as for the children, God has made
special provisions for them in heaven due to their
innocence, "but unfortunately", they're still
subjected to the wickedness of this world, and will
have to suffer as a consequence of its actions,
nevertheless, God is especially concerned for their
souls, which is why **"Gays and Lesbians"** should
never raise children, as it exposes them to
(**unrighteousness and immorality**), which is a
very serious matter with God, because if you choose
to send your own soul to **"Hell"**, *"that's one thing"*,
but influencing children in that direction *"is another
whole matter entirely!"*

And anyone who **"oppresses, distorts_or perverts"**
children, are all of the same accord, which means
that **Homosexuals** are equivalent to **Pedophiles**,
whom are equivalent to all other abusers of
children, due to the fact that they all abuse children,
"just in different ways".

For example, the types of abuse:

- The Pedophile (**morally, physically,
  sexually**).

227

- Gays and Lesbians (**morally, sexually, socially, domestically**).
- All other Abusers (**physically, mentally, spiritually, emotionally**).

So Jesus warns those who abuse little children that there will be "**Hell**" to pay, (**Literally**).
In fact, God has declared the spirit of a child to be so sacred that he requires every adult to humble themselves as children, seeing that a child is innocent in all that he or she does, and therefore are established by God in the kingdom of heaven, as Jesus explaines below:

Matthew 18: (KJV)

12 And Jesus called a little child unto him, and set him in the midst of them, **3** And said, Verily I say unto you, Except ye be converted, and become as little children, ye shall not enter into the kingdom of heaven. **4** Whosoever therefore shall humble himself as this little child, the same is greatest in the kingdom of heaven. **5** And whoso shall receive one such little child in my name receiveth me. **6** But whoso shall offend one of these little ones which believe in me, it were better for him that a millstone were hanged about his neck, and *that* he were drowned in the depth of the sea. **7** Woe unto the world because of offences! for it must needs be that offences come; but woe to that man by whom the offence cometh!

So here we can see that God doesn't take it lightly when children are mistreated, nor will he be sparing in his justice and punishment on those who commit such acts, as stated by Jesus:
"But whoso shall offend one of these little ones which believe in me, it were better for him that a millstone were hanged about his neck, and *that* he were drowned in the depth of the sea". So not only does God detest the abuse and mistreatment of children, but he's equally offended by the mistreatment of those who humble themselves before him as if they were a child.
Also, when Jesus says: **"woe unto the world because of offences"** he's saying that there will always be trouble in this present world due to the wickedness and unrighteousness of mankind, (*which is another good explanation of why things happen to innocent children*), then he goes on to say: **" for it must needs be that offences come"**, now what this means is that the wheels were set into motion over a thousand years ago by God to correct the behavior of mankind, because God saw that mankind's nature was continually evil, so ever since, this world has been on a collision course that will lead to destruction, and then the end!

Jesus then concludes by warning the world: "**but woe to that man by whom the offence cometh**", so what he's saying here is that those whom are responsible for down spiral of the world, such as:

(Gays and lesbians, Pedophiles, Rapist, Abusers, Murders, Corrupt individuals, fornicators, adulator, thieves, etc)

all will have Hell to pay," *literally*!"
And in this particular verse when Jesus says "**that man**", he's actually referring to women as well, he's speaking in the context of **mankind**, which means human beings, it's a biblical term that's often used where you will find the words (**men and man**) that actually refers to **mankind**. So in this particular case he's speaking of "**men and women**" whom are wicked or unrighteous,

And here's a more in-depth look at some of the offences and behavior of those listed above that have contributed to down spiral of the world, which leads to "**Hell**" (**Eternal Damnation**)......

Romans 1: (KJV)

24 Wherefore God also gave them up to uncleanness through the lusts of their own hearts, to dishonour their own bodies between themselves:
25 Who changed the truth of God into a lie, and

worshipped and served the creature more than the Creator, who is blessed for ever. Amen.

26 For this cause God gave them up unto vile affections: for even their women did change the natural use into that which is against nature: **27** And likewise also the men, leaving the natural use of the woman, burned in their lust one toward another; men with men working that which is unseemly, and receiving in themselves that recompence of their error which was meet.

28 And even as they did not like to retain God in *their* knowledge, God gave them over to a reprobate mind, to do those things which are not convenient; **29** Being filled with all unrighteousness, fornication, wickedness, covetousness, maliciousness; full of envy, murder, debate, deceit, malignity; whisperers, **30** Backbiters, haters of God, despiteful, proud, boasters, inventors of evil things, disobedient to parents, **31** Without understanding, covenantbreakers, without natural affection, implacable, unmerciful: **32** Who knowing the judgment of God, that they which commit such things are worthy of death, not only do the same, but have pleasure in them that do them.

Notice that in <u>Romans 1:26</u> the bible is speaking specifically of (**Lesbians**), as it states:
"For this cause God gave them up unto vile affections: for even their women did change the natural use into that which is against nature". So it describes women leaving the natural use for men and turning to one another for vile affections, (**Homosexuality**).

And <u>Romans 1: 27</u> speaks specifically of (**Gay men**), stating:
"And likewise also the men, leaving the natural use of the woman, burned in their lust one toward another; men with men working that which is unseemly, and receiving in themselves that recompence of their error which was meet". This of course describes (**Men**), and how they turned from being with women to be with one another, (**Homosexuality**), as it stated: **"men with men"** against nature. And the bible goes on to explain that due to the fact that people choose these (**perversions**), and actually **"lust "**for them, God gives them up to these perversions, *"and no longer accepts them"*, which means that if God no longer accepts you, then he no longer accept your (**prayers**) or your (**praise**), nor will he (**protect you, heal you, or show you mercy and forgiveness**), unless you repent.

"So how then" do you think that you can <u>pray to God</u>, <u>worship God</u>, or <u>have a church of God</u>, if you are living these lifestyles that serve Satan, "which God deplores", and has given you up for? That means that on top of everything else, you're also living a lie, and are as one of those described in <u>Romans 1: 25</u>: **"Who changed the truth of God into a lie"**.

And also notice that in <u>1 Corinthians 6:9</u>, it states: **"nor effeminate, nor abusers of themselves with mankind"** may enter into the Kingdom God, and the term **(effeminate)** refers to men who act **(feminine, womanly or gay)**. And as for those who **(abuse themselves with mankind)** we know that this can be both, *"male and female"*, and refers to any inappropriate behavior which results between two or more individuals.

These are all the acts of those who have chosen to remove God from their lives.

So for those of you who have chosen to remove God from **(government, politics, schools, homes, and your lives)**, he accepts your rejection, and likewise *"REJECTS YOU AS WELL!"*

1 Corinthians 6: (KJV)

9 Know ye not that the unrighteous shall not inherit the kingdom of God? Be not deceived: neither fornicators, nor idolaters, nor adulterers, nor effeminate, nor abusers of themselves with mankind, **10** Nor thieves, nor covetous, nor drunkards, nor revilers, nor extortioners, shall inherit the kingdom of God.

So due to the fact that you've taken time to check out this book, shows that you have an interest in the truth, which means that righteousness is within you, even if you choose not to accept it. And if you should begin to feel pain, remorse or shame, it's because righteousness is in you, and your conscious is still alive. "Apparently" you aren't as one of those who have seared their conscious with a hot iron. But on the other hand, those who aren't moved, and feel no shame, remorse or pain, are as one of those who have seared their conscious with a hot iron, and probably won't turn back, "but again" that isn't for any of us to say, because all things are possible with God. So be it as it may, to each his or her own respectfully, take some time to think, don't go into despair, or become irate, because it isn't you, but the sin that God hates. And if the truth be told, you're not any less of a person than anyone else, even though many will try and make you feel that way, but as they condemn you, it is their own soul which will be required in hell. Now with that being said, those who serve God or seek to serve God, are required by God to reject homosexuality, but with the utmost respect to the individuals, and

234

anything outside of this is unacceptable and not of God, nor does this person represent God.

I DEDICATE THIS BOOK TO THE WORLD

"So to all, "I hope you choose righteousness", because you deserve the best!"

This book was not written to judge or denigrate, because it's God who passes judgment which this book clearly states, but it does support his laws which it also demonstrates, and exposes the truth in homosexuality and foolish debates. So by now you should understand we have choices to make, and you're completely free of will in the path you'll take, so you can no longer point the finger of blame, making all kinds of excuses instead of using your brain, knowing deep inside that it's you who prefer to sin, so if a change is going to come it has to come from within, because God doesn't except our excuses and lies, his mercy is for those who repent and not for those who deny.

"God is real!"

Titus 2: (KJV)

11: For the grace of God that bringeth salvation hath appeared to all men, 12: Teaching us that, denying ungodliness and worldly lusts, we should live soberly, righteously, and godly, in this present world;

PRAISE BE TO GOD

JEHOVAH GOD

THE GOD OF ABRAHAM, ISAAC AND JACOB

"CLEMY'S GOD"

THE AUTHOR

A man,

"by no means perfect", but one whom has humbled himself before God, such as Solomon, Ezra, Jeremiah and Job, to know the righteousness of a matter, and to apply it, a man whom God has chastened, and continues to chasten with knowledge and wisdom, in hopes that I may be enlightened, and enlighten others.

CLEMY LEE

www.ingramcontent.com/pod-product-compliance
Lightning Source LLC
LaVergne TN
LVHW051502080426
835509LV00017B/1879

9780692933961